Simply Put

Simply Put

Why Clear Messages Win —and How to Design Them

Ben Guttmann

BK

Berrett–Koehler Publishers, Inc.

Berrett-Koehler Publishers, Inc.
1333 Broadway, Suite 1000
Oakland, CA 94612-1921
Tel: (510) 817-2277
Fax: (510) 817-2278
www.bkconnection.com

ORDERING INFORMATION
Quantity sales. Special discounts are available on quantity purchases by corporations, associations, and others. For details, contact the "Special Sales Department" at the Berrett-Koehler address above.
Individual sales. Berrett-Koehler publications are available through most bookstores. They can also be ordered directly from Berrett-Koehler: Tel: (800) 929-2929; Fax: (802) 864-7626; www.bkconnection.com.
Orders for college textbook / course adoption use. Please contact Berrett-Koehler: Tel: (800) 929-2929; Fax: (802) 864-7626.

Distributed to the U.S. trade and internationally by Penguin Random House Publisher Services.

Berrett-Koehler and the BK logo are registered trademarks of Berrett-Koehler Publishers, Inc.

Printed in the United States of America

Berrett-Koehler books are printed on long-lasting acid-free paper. When it is available, we choose paper that has been manufactured by environmentally responsible processes. These may include using trees grown in sustainable forests, incorporating recycled paper, minimizing chlorine in bleaching, or recycling the energy produced at the paper mill.

Library of Congress Cataloging-in-Publication Data

Names: Guttmann, Ben, author.
Title: Simply put : why clear messages win—and how to design them / Ben
   Guttmann.
Description: First edition. | Oakland, CA : Berrett-Koehler Publishers,
   [2023] | Includes bibliographical references and index.
Identifiers: LCCN 2023009697 (print) | LCCN 2023009698 (ebook) | ISBN
   9781523004683 (paperback) | ISBN 9781523004690 (pdf) | ISBN
   9781523004706 (epub) | ISBN 9781523004713 (audio)
Subjects: LCSH: Business communication. | Interpersonal communication. |
   Simplicity.
Classification: LCC HF5718 .G88 2023 (print) | LCC HF5718 (ebook) | DDC
   658.4/5—dc23/eng/20230602
LC record available at https://lccn.loc.gov/2023009697
LC ebook record available at https://lccn.loc.gov/2023009698

First Edition

31 30 29 28 27 26 25 24 23   10 9 8 7 6 5 4 3 2 1

Book producer: PeopleSpeak
Text designer: Reider Books
Cover designer: Matt Avery

For Stephania

Contents

Preface

L ook, I fully realize the irony here. This is a 208-page book about how to say things simply. It doesn't really seem like I took my own advice, now does it?

This whole thing started while I was trying to answer a basic question that I've been attempting to solve my entire career—something that clients would ask me while I was running a marketing agency or my college students ask when I'm teaching them the ropes.

"Why do some messages work when others don't?"

The question is simple. And as it turns out, the answer is also, quite literally, *simple*. That first part isn't particularly revelatory. If all you want to know is the top-line answer, that's it: simple messages are more effective than complicated ones. If that's enough for you, hopefully I caught you before you checked out and saved you a few bucks.

But I noticed something funny while investigating simplicity. It turns out that simple isn't so simple—and it sure as hell isn't easy. We can pretty easily know *what* works just by using common sense, but it's a different thing to know *why* things work, and it's another thing altogether to know *how* to create messages that work.

There's science and there's history. There are lessons from the world's most captivating leaders and most innovative companies. There are tools that we can all use to harness the power of simplicity to connect and communicate.

And that's how we ended up here, with a whole book about simplicity. Let's get started.

Why Simple?

Perfection is achieved, not when there is nothing more to add,
but when there is nothing left to take away.

—Antoine de Saint-Exupéry

Think about the most powerful messages you've ever heard. Picture the most life-changing piece of advice passed down from a mentor, the most stirring call to action in a stump speech, or the stickiest slogan ever splashed across a commercial.

We've all been told to "not judge a book by its cover," to "not count your chickens before they hatch," and that "Rome wasn't built in a day." My personal favorite bit of received wisdom, essentially a piece of meta-advice, is "all advice is autobiographical."

Maybe for you what comes to mind is something political, such as Patrick Henry's revolutionary "Give me liberty, or give me death!" or, more recently, Barack Obama's "Yes We Can." In the halls of great marketing, you might remember Apple's "Think Different" or Nike's "Just Do It."

Take a moment to think about the other few thousand messages you heard in the past twenty-four hours—such as ads, warnings, instructions, or even instances you sought out, such as articles, social media posts, or stories. How many of them do you remember? How much of what you say do other people remember? Do they actually even hear what you're saying?

Regardless if these messages are trying to get your dollars, your votes, or just your thoughts, the most effective messages all share one thing. They are simple.

Simple ideas stick. Simple messages win.

We live in a world of great complexity, with countless devices and apps buzzing, beeping, and demanding our whiplashed attention during every waking hour (and some of the sleeping ones). Though we know this, and we know as a receiver that clear messages capture our focus, we have an awfully hard time getting simple when we're the ones doing the talking. How many slides of dense bullet points were in your last presentation? How many acronyms did you throw out in your last client meeting?

It hurts when we have something we want to say that doesn't get through. Communication problems are cited as the single most common factor in divorce. Employees who feel ignored at work are less satisfied and less productive. Voters routinely complain about politicians ignoring their voices, and customers rage at companies who refuse to listen to them.

And all of this is before we even count the billions of dollars businesses spend each year on advertising that falls flat.

This book is for anybody who has something to say but is struggling to get heard. It's for entrepreneurs and executives who have a product to sell, for visionary leaders who want to change their communities, and for storytellers of all stripes who have something they want to share with the world. Together we'll examine why clear, straightforward messages break through and how we can get better at doing the hard work of getting simple.

Why Simple Wins

Over the past ten years of building and running a marketing agency, and nearly as long teaching marketing at my alma mater, Baruch College, I've been obsessed with trying to figure out why we do the things that we do—and how we can be better at breaking through all that noise to tell the world our stories. I've worked with some of the greatest brands in business and some of the world's most influential scientists, executives, and writers. I've conducted hundreds of user and customer interviews, and I've talked with dozens of the most successful marketing minds working today. Everywhere I go, I've been trying to find the secret recipe that separates messages that work from those that don't.

The fact that I was on this quest, though, was all a little embarrassing, to be honest. Clients would pay us big contracts and students would look to me for some sort of professorial wisdom, but I didn't really understand the fundamental nature of this question. When I'd ask other professionals, I would find out that I'm far from alone.

This question stuck with me enough to peel back the layers and write a whole book about the answer. This question defines so much of our personal and professional lives: "Why do some messages work when others don't?"

A straightforward claim of "1,000 songs in your pocket" helped Apple revolutionize the music industry with the iPod. But the clearance rack is full of products that couldn't connect with customers in the same way.

Messages without fluff helped propel both Donald Trump and Alexandria Ocasio-Cortez to the height of influence in American politics. But lots of also-rans haven't moved voters the same way.

The blunt "truth" anti-smoking campaign helped drive down teen tobacco use, saving both thousands of lives and piles of cash in public health costs. But lots of other well-intentioned campaigns haven't changed behavior in the same way.

Successful messages all share something in common. And it's something we can all learn.

Whether you're looking to move millions of dollars in products or for a way to better get your ideas across in your work and personal life, embracing the power of simple messages can help you get to where you want to go. As we begin this journey, we'll first look at the surprising science and history behind this powerful idea.

We'll examine the eye-opening limitations of our attention, memory, and cognition and how the finicky brains *Homo sapiens* have fail us in an ever busier and more demanding world. We like to think we're pretty smart, but ultimately we fail to notice a lot of the world around us, we fail to remember much of what we do notice, and we often don't even know the stuff we think we know. Set loose in a society of constant connectivity and infinite scrolls, and where our attention is regularly being sold to the highest bidder, we can easily see how and why most messages don't get heard.

We'll then see why embracing simplicity helps us overcome these obstacles. We'll learn what the world's best communicators have known for thousands of years and see how today's consumers pay a premium for simplicity.

You've likely heard this idea before. Seven centuries ago, Franciscan friar William of Occam argued, roughly, that the simplest theory is usually the right answer, which would later be named Occam's razor. In just the last few years, more and more of us have been embracing "less is more" concepts, such as minimalism, as we seek refuge against a noisier and louder world.

But what exactly do we mean by simple? Here's the definition we'll use:

Simple: When a message is easily perceived, understood, and acted upon

What makes something easily perceived, understood, and acted on? These simple messages have five attributes: beneficial, focused, salient, empathetic, and minimal. We'll explore each of these principles and how we can put them to work throughout this book.

Finally, after we understand the battle we're fighting, we'll learn why we so often lose it. We'll meet our nemesis: the complicated.

We often have a bias to add, an easy retreat into complexity, and a fear of taking big swings. The complicated is attractive because it doesn't require sacrifice or hard choices. But, as we'll see in disasters large and small, when we cower into the path of least resistance and fail to communicate clearly, we can pay a devastating price.

How to Get Simple

Now that we know the challenges and how vital simplicity is in our mission to connect, we're going to dispel the mystique and show how anybody can use this powerful idea in their own work and lives. In the second half of this book, we'll pull out the five-part tool kit for developing simple messages, empowering you to break through and become a world-class leader and communicator.

We'll look first at the power of orienting our language to highlight benefits instead of features, providing a research-backed model that can help anybody better structure their communication (and that the most influential brands and leaders already use).

We'll investigate how to develop individual and collective focus, slaying the dreaded "Frankenstein idea" while navigating the dicey politics of saying more by saying less—a tightrope act that takes courage and creative leadership.

We'll then learn some not-so-secret techniques that help us make our message sharper, embracing constraints to stand out from the crowd.

We'll use empathy and research to help us get out of our own way, blow up our assumptions, and connect with our audience where they are.

We'll vigorously cut away the BS, arriving at a winning message free of distractions.

By the end of this book, you'll be able to slash through the dangerous thickets of fluff and jargon, get to the point, and get your ideas heard.

Senders and Receivers

In this book, we're going to, appropriately, simplify the way we label the two halves of the communications equation:

+ *Senders* are those with the message. Senders can be advertisers, executives, politicians, faith leaders, parents, teachers, advocates, regulators, or anybody with something to say.
+ *Receivers* are those who are the intended recipients of the message. Receivers can be customers, voters, donors, users, citizens, policymakers, spouses, or anybody else whom we want to connect with.

We all wear both these hats, and often at the same time. Indeed, we're receivers far more often than we're senders. Even the biggest gasbags among us still listen more than they speak.

But this book is about how to be a better sender. Senders are the ones with a mission, and they are the ones that need to do the work to make sure that their communication works. Being a sender is tough—it's stressful and taxing, and we're often just not very good at it. That's where we need help.

The other shorthand we'll use repeatedly is the term *message* to encapsulate any piece of information that needs to be sent by a sender to a receiver as shown in figure I.1. Messages are ideas and concepts. Most of the time, they are made up of words but are better thought of as being represented by words, images, and other elements rather than being the words themselves. Messages can be advertisements, rallying calls, memos, warnings, lessons, stories, or anything else that we want to communicate.

We're going to talk about words a lot because that is how we bring this fuzzy idea into our reality. But this is not a copy-writing manual or style guide. It's about taking that formless idea in your head and shaping it into a message that gets from the sender to the receiver.

When your message is too big and expansive, it doesn't make it out of that head of yours. It gets stuck.

Figure I.1. This is a book about how to design better messages—which can take many forms.

When your message is shapeless and unformed, it leaks out but can't be caught by the receiver. It slips right through their fingers.

When your message is clunky and clouded, it arrives but doesn't have a home. It gets put to the side and forgotten in a pile of clutter.

We're going to call all those sins *complicated*. Complicated ideas don't work. Only when you simplify your message does it get out, get caught, and get used.

Two Secrets before We Begin

While my background is in marketing, and many of the most prolific senders are those with advertising dollars, this book isn't only for marketers. It's a wake-up call and a guide for anybody with something they want to tell others.

However, it just so happens that our industry is the one that most folks call on when they find themselves in that very situation. This is what marketers do: we tell the world the idea we want people to know about, and if we're good at that, hopefully we get people to take the action that we want them to take.

Today we're all marketers in some form. We go about our lives trying to persuade colleagues of our great idea, cajole our kids into doing their chores, or get our friends to donate to our fundraiser. So, since you're part of the team, I figure it would be good to let you in on a couple of trade secrets before we go on with the rest of this book.

The first one is not something you're going to see in a lot of agency pitches or college textbooks, but this truth is so fundamental that the whole industry wouldn't exist if it weren't the case. Here it is: nobody cares.

Nobody cares about what you are trying to tell them, and they especially don't care about what you're trying to sell them. Nobody wants to watch your commercial or visit your website. Almost every advertisement that anybody has ever seen has been against their will. The entire industry is an uphill battle against apathy and disinterest.

To help illustrate why this is the case, there's this beautiful little word that I've always loved that virally makes its way around the internet every few months, *sonder*. At first, it seems German (they have a word for everything), but it was actually coined by blogger John Koenig on his Tumblr site *The Dictionary of Obscure Sorrows*.[1] Here's his original definition:

> *Sonder*
>
> *n.* the realization that each random passerby is living a life as vivid and complex as your own—populated with their own ambitions, friends, routines, worries and inherited craziness—an epic story that continues invisibly around you like an anthill sprawling deep underground, with elaborate passageways to thousands of other lives that you'll never know existed, in which you might appear only once, as an extra sipping coffee in the background, as a blur of traffic passing on the highway, as a lighted window at dusk.

This idea—that every light in the city skyline or car on the freeway represents a whole, full life—is a ticklish, awe-inspiring concept that helps us grasp the task at hand. To us, we're the main characters of the story. Everybody should care what I, the protagonist, have to say. I'm excited by my new product, therefore everybody else must be as well!

But when we understand that everybody else is out there living through their own rich, vivid story, and to them, *you* are just that inverted flickering face in the passing train, we begin to see the challenge. Everybody you want to talk to is busy, and they woke up today perfectly fine without your product or message. They're preoccupied worrying about the pesky leak in their roof, working to meet that big upcoming deadline, or daydreaming about next week's beach vacation. The precious time and attention they have to give to you is just a slim window, if you're lucky to get any at all. People care about lots of things all the time—but they aren't waiting for you to come with your message.

This reality is ultimately why simplicity is so important. Like a sharpened spear pierces a suit of armor, we need a sharpened message to pierce the fog and be heard.

The second industry secret is about how the business of marketing itself works. For all the scaffolding we put up that makes our work seem professional, technical, or even scientific, the entire act of marketing boils down to just two things: what you say and how you say it.

A lot of ink, airtime, and pixels have gone into the "how you say it" part of the pairing. This half of the equation includes television commercials and newspaper ads on the more traditional side and then Instagram posts and Google search ads on the more contemporary, digital side. Most of the people in this business work on these aspects—this job is essential, and often demanding, but it's also only half of what we need to do to successfully market. This all is the vessel.

This book is not about that. Especially in today's environment, how we do those tactical bits of marketing changes far too fast, and frankly you're better off learning how by popping onto YouTube or Reddit and following the latest trends. And (to be honest) picking up these tools is not all that hard if you're willing to put the work in.

Instead, this book is about that deceptively difficult first part of the equation, how we fill that vessel. This book is about helping us figure out what we say, and knowing how to do that effectively helps us regardless if we've ever set foot in an advertising agency.

This skill is more important today than it's ever been. First, we have to deal with the onslaught of advertising we discussed a moment ago. Over the course of the more than thirteen hours the average American adult spends consuming some form of media each day, we might see thousands of ads competing for our attention.[2] Cutting through the noise and getting heard is harder than ever.

But another trend is ringing alarm bells throughout the marketing and technology industries, and it signals an epochal shift in how the internet works. For the last twenty or so years, the vessel that has been most effective in spreading your message has been some form of targeted online advertising. We've all seen these ads, and we've all clicked on them (and I know, I used to create them). On one level, there are the ones that are pretty straightforward: if you like hiking posts on Facebook, you'll see ads trying to sell you boots. But we've also all been subjected to what are called *remarketing* or *retargeting* ads, where you may have visited a website looking at a particular pair of boots, and then ads for those boots will follow you around for a few weeks. The reason you're nodding along in recognition of both types of ads is that they are crazy effective, and because of that, Facebook and the like have made billions of dollars serving them up to you.

Ads like these require a form of digital tracking, often in the form of a small file known as a *cookie* that identifies who you are when you visit different places on the web. But here's the problem: tracking is dying. Apple, Google, and Mozilla have all taken steps over the last couple of years to drastically limit the ability of ad platforms to peek over your shoulder as you move around the internet, and the results are beginning to show. After they released their first numbers revealing the effect of these changes, Facebook's parent company Meta's stock plummeted by more than 20 percent in a single day. The era of just hitting you over the head with ads until you reluctantly click the Buy button is over.

That tool was a crutch, and now it's gone. The type of blunt force marketing that people like me used to run for the last decade won't work in the next decade. The reason I'm writing this book today is to prepare all of us for that future, regardless if you've ever run an ad.

In the next era, where marketers can't just get a shortcut to success by pushing and pulling the levers of hypertargeting, persuasion and communication professionals need to embrace a return to the fundamentals of telling a good message. Technologies change, but humans don't. The recipe for effective communication is the same as it has been since we first started writing on stone tablets five thousand years ago. That's what this book is about: why simple messages win and how we can be better at designing them.

The old models are broken. But as we'll soon see, they're not the only thing that isn't working.

PART 1

Why Simple Wins

1

Our Stupid Brains
in Our Busy World

To pay attention, this is our endless and proper work.

—Mary Oliver

How do you tie your shoes?

You've probably tied your shoes tens of thousands of times since you first learned to do so in grade school. The act is muscle memory by now. But could you explain it to somebody else?

How does a flush toilet work?

You've maybe flushed a toilet a hundred thousand times in your life. This machine is pretty simple, just a piece of curvy porcelain, a handle, and a few moving bits inside. No wires or chips are involved. But can you explain what happens when you push down that lever?

What did you eat for lunch two Tuesdays ago?

You were there, and it wasn't that long ago. You walked into the restaurant and placed the order after scanning the menu, or you packed it up on the kitchen counter earlier that morning. You took a bite, hopefully enjoyed it, and cleaned up the scraps after. But do you remember exactly what it was?

These questions aren't difficult, or at least they shouldn't be. But we all struggle with them. We can't remember most of what's scurried across our attention, we don't know as much as we thought we did, and we struggle with communicating even the things that we are the most experienced in. Our minds aren't computers recording and processing everything in perfect precision—they are imperfect, fleshy machines.

Despite these limitations, we get along pretty okay most of the time. We tie our shoes, flush toilets, and eat lunch without any issues most days of the week. We're good, talented users of the world around us. We run into trouble, though, when we're thrust into the other role: when we become somebody who has something to say, build, or share. That's when everything breaks down.

Most of our communications rely on a foundational idea: we are smart, caring, rational actors who pay attention and understand what other people are saying—in all ways all the time. But because of our nature and the world we've built around us, that simply isn't the case.

This is the problem, this is why so many of our messages don't get through. To put it bluntly, we're stupid, and we're busy.

The Problem with Us

The beautiful truth is that we are imperfect beings. Stories aren't interesting without conflict, sweet doesn't taste as good without salty, and life would be both boring and stressful if our brains worked perfectly every single time.

We know this because a handful of people in the world *do* notice and remember pretty much everything. A rare condition known as *hyperthymesia* allows these individuals to look back on their lives as a vivid movie, picturing the people, places, and things that make up their autobiography in the same way you or I might scroll through a photo gallery. While this memory is not perfect, it's pretty damn close. Having this condition means recalling birthdays, weddings, breakups, and funerals all with the same level of detail. One patient describes it as "nonstop, uncontrollable and totally exhausting."[1] It's not ideal.

We ignore and forget because it helps us live our lives. But when we're somebody with a message that we don't want to be ignored or forgotten, this biological programming can feel like an insurmountable obstacle. To understand the territory, let's tour some of our biggest trouble spots.

We Don't Notice Most Things

In an aggressively beige, nondescript hallway, six students move about in a circular pattern. Half of them are dressed in white shirts, and the others wear black shirts. Each color-co-ordinated team passes a basketball back and forth among themselves, smiling as they perform the demonstration in front of a closed bank of elevator doors.

A few seconds after they begin, an actor in a gorilla suit walks through the group, stares at the camera and pounds its chest, then heads off in the other direction. The students keep passing the ball.

Weird, right? That must have caught your attention.

Not necessarily. When the researchers who designed this test showed the scene to participants, tasking them before it played to count how many passes the team in white makes, only 42 percent of viewers noticed the gorilla. Incredibly, most viewers counted the fifteen passes the team made and saw nothing out of the ordinary.

This famous study by psychologists Daniel Simons and Christopher Chabris illustrates the puzzling phenomenon of inattentional blindness, where we fail to notice something in plain sight.[2] When we're in a busy environment, distracted by a task or other stimuli competing for our attention, we'll miss something right in front of us—even if it is an eight hundred-pound gorilla.

There is nothing special about that gorilla suit or basketball. This "blindness" happens *all of the time.*

When we're engrossed in a conversation while behind the wheel, we'll fail to see the car that "came out of nowhere." When we're so hung up on a particularly tough level of a video game, we miss our spouse entering the room asking about dinner plans. When we're crunching on a work deadline in the airport lounge, we'll go deaf to the blaring last-call announcement for our departing flight.

Nothing is wrong with our eyes or ears. Our retinas faithfully pick up these sights and feed the sensations through our optic nerve to the cerebral cortex. Our eardrums vibrate and pulse electrical signals up our auditory nerve. But often, something right there can fail to register in our consciousness. Instead, our brain takes shortcuts, filling in the blanks with what we expect to be there and getting on with whatever else we were doing.

Subconsciously filtering out unnecessary details has been evolutionarily advantageous in our development. Imagine how exhausting it would be to consciously process and consider every single thing that comes before us. Our ancient ancestors would have sat around, pondering and reviewing each blade of grass, quickly becoming a leisurely lunch for a hungry predator lurking behind a tree. But as any marketer who's burned through an ad budget with vanishingly small click rates to show for it will tell you, this propensity to filter is bad if you're trying to get somebody's attention.

The psychologist Simons, who ran that gorilla study, later said, "One conclusion of the inattentional blindness work has been that we see far less of our world than we think we do. . . . We feel like we've got all the details of the things going on around us. But my bet is that most of the time people are really focused on one goal at a time."[3]

By some estimates, we take in 11 million bits of information every second through our senses, but our conscious brain has the bandwidth to attend to about only 0.0004 percent of them.[4] Long before we measured information in bits, pioneering nineteenth-century psychologist William James wrote, "Millions of items of the outward order are present to my senses which never properly enter into my experience. Why? Because they have no *interest* for me. My experience is what I agree to attend to. Only those items which I notice shape my mind—without selective interest, experience is an utter chaos."[5]

Our attention is precious and finite, and we prefer to spend it on what matters to us. We notice information that is tied to our goals and helps us survive and thrive, but to do that, we subconsciously filter out the inputs that don't matter as much. And often, that means failing to notice most of the messages bombarding us at any given moment.

We Don't Remember Most of Everything

Late on a Friday night in December 2010, a frantic young man named Aaron Scheerhoorn showed up at the door of a Houston nightclub.[6] He opened his shirt, revealing a bloody stab wound to the bouncers, and begged urgently to enter the club for safety. Despite these pleas, the doormen never let him in, soon allowing the large man following him to catch up and stab him again. After running away through a nearby parking lot, Scheerhoorn was stabbed several more times by the attacker, whom passersby saw eventually get up and calmly walk away. Later that night, Aaron Scheerhoorn was declared dead at the nearby hospital.

Over the course of the gruesome evening, eight witnesses saw the attacker. The next day, one of them reported that he spotted a man who he thought looked like the killer. The police tracked down this suspect's name from his car: Lydell Grant.

Detectives shared photos of Grant with other witnesses. Two of the bouncers said that was him. Two of the patrons said that was him. The passersby from the parking lot said that was him. In total, six of the eight witnesses immediately identified Grant as the attacker they saw that night. The police had their man.

Several days later, Grant was pulled over, arrested, and charged with first-degree murder. The police found some other fuzzy evidence: a ski mask and knife in his trunk and some indeterminate male DNA scraped from under his fingernails. But the six witnesses were all the prosecutors needed to make their case. Two years later, on December 6, 2012, Grant was found guilty—and sentenced to life in prison.

Lydell Grant did not kill Aaron Scheerhoorn.

On the strength of DNA evidence, and with the help of the Innocence Project of Texas, Grant was released in 2019, and his conviction was soon formally overturned. The real killer, Jermarico Carter, confessed shortly after being arrested. The false conviction that stole almost a decade of Grant's life was nearly entirely based on the faulty memory of six witnesses.

Sadly, this case is not a rare exception. Ronald Cotton was falsely convicted of rape and sentenced to life in prison in 1985 on flawed eyewitness testimony, only to be exonerated by DNA evidence in 1995. Ryan Matthews spent five years on death row for a crime he didn't commit after nearby witnesses falsely identified him in 1999. According to the Innocence Project, 69 percent of DNA exonerations in the United States involve misidentification from eyewitnesses, and 32 percent of those involved multiple misidentifications by different witnesses.[7]

Even when the stakes are life and death, we have a hard time remembering what we saw, what we heard, or what happened.

In our brains, we have four forms of memory: sensory, short-term, working, and long-term memory.[8] Sensory memory is the first, exceedingly brief store of information that comes in from our senses. It's basically the gatekeeper that filters everything around us and selects what makes it through to our consciousness. All the stimuli from the world around us goes in and out of this station of memory in less than a second. This type of memory is what we talked about in the previous section.

If information makes it through this attentional filter, it arrives in our short-term memory. Our short-term memory is where we keep details at the top of our minds as we're thinking and doing things in the world around us, such as the last sentence you read or a phone number you're dialing.

Overlapping with short-term memory is our working memory, where we access, hold, and manipulate information to plan and carry out behavior. Working memory is how we put short-term memory to use, such as following recipe instructions, solving a math problem, or engaging in debate.

These three stages are also small and brief in storage.

In an influential 1956 study, Harvard psychologist George Miller discovered a consistent limit on short-term memory.[9] It didn't matter if people were trying to recall numbers, sounds, letters, or words. Everywhere he looked, he found our short-term memory limit was, as he titled the paper, "The Magical Number Seven, Plus or Minus Two." According to Miller, we can reliably hold only about seven "chunks" of information in our head at any one time.

Subsequent research has pushed this estimate down to four. And still other studies have shown that this capacity might be better represented by time: we can typically recall only as much as what we can verbalize in roughly two seconds.[10] Either way we cut it, this capacity is vanishingly tiny. In the short run, our attention and our capacity to retain information are much more limited than we would like to think.

Then we face another problem: our memory decays—fast. Unless we go out of our way to re-up its shelf life, new information is gone within about fifteen to thirty seconds. This is why you can't easily remember the exact line that character said a few scenes back when watching a movie or what else was on the menu at the restaurant by the time your food arrives. Our brains processed the information, made use of it, and then tossed it aside after it served its purpose. Some stuff makes its way to our long-term memory storage, but the vast majority doesn't. Forgetting, by clearing out the unnecessary mental clutter, isn't the exception; it's the default.

Largely because so much doesn't clear these dual hurdles of attention and storage, we must question the reliability of what does. Leading researcher Elizabeth F. Loftus says that remembering is "more akin to putting puzzle pieces together than retrieving a video recording."[11] Each time we call up a memory, we're not pressing play, we're reconstructing it—and we're susceptible to making mistakes while we do.

The eyewitnesses in the story of Lydell Grant and the other wrongly convicted exonerees above were wrong, but that doesn't necessarily mean they were ill intentioned. Like most of us, their memory was far from photographic, and when they were called on to use it in a moment of incredibly high stakes, it failed them and everybody involved. As they tried to reconstruct a hazy memory, their mind put a few pieces together, filled in the rest with context clues, and said, "Okay, good enough."

These witnesses were operating in high-stress, real-life conditions, often in the dark and from a distance, not memorizing a photograph in a dedicated study session. Only so much information was received, and even less made it to storage. When put head to head with a pushy prosecutor looking to score a conviction, their imperfect, limited, *human* memory didn't stand a chance.

We Don't Know What We Think We Know

Even when we notice something, even when we remember something, do we actually know anything? The truth is that we all know lots of things, and we get through most of our days just fine—but we also think we know a lot more than we really do.

Let's go back to flush toilets, which we mentioned at the beginning of this chapter. Details of your personal hygiene aside, you've likely been flushing away all your life, making this device one of your longest-running and most intimate technological interactions. But if you were sent back in time five hundred years, could you build one?

Unless you're a plumber, if you answered yes, you've likely just fallen for another one of our mental shortcomings: the illusion of explanatory depth. This phenomenon is where people feel they understand complex topics, ideas, and systems more than they actually do.

In the original Yale study identifying this concept, graduate students were asked to estimate how much they understood how a series of devices or systems work, from speedometers and the US Supreme Court to, yes, flush toilets.[12] After they rated their knowledge, the participants were told to write a detailed explanation of each idea and afterward rerate their level of understanding.

The results: nearly every single participant struggled with their explanations and lowered their rating of their own knowledge after doing so. When replicated with undergraduates or beyond the tony campuses of the Ivy League, the same results occurred. We don't know what we think we know.

This illusion is related to another common quirk of overestimation: the Dunning-Kruger effect. This well-known cognitive bias is when inexperienced or incompetent people tend to overrate their ability or performance. We see this all around us: bad students think they're getting better grades than they are, and poor chess players think they are more likely to win than they are. In a particularly jarring example, 12 percent of average, everyday British men believe they can score a point against Serena Williams, the greatest player of all time, in a game of tennis. Coincidentally, that's the same percentage of overconfident Americans who somehow think they could defeat a wolf in a hand-to-hand fight.[13]

Taken together, these shortcomings play out every time we try to communicate, as shown in figure 1.1. At every step of the process of taking information from out in the world and getting it into our thick heads, we face problems. Each sliver of attention and focus is a tiny miracle.

The Problem with Everything Else

All these bugs may make it seem like we're pretty faulty machines. But we're not broken any more than a fish is broken

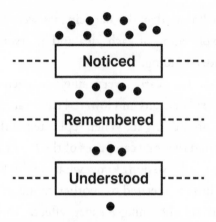

Figure 1.1. Some stuff gets noticed, fewer things get remembered, and only a small fraction of things get understood.

for being unable to climb a tree or a snail because it can't fly—they just aren't built for these situations. We're imperfect, but it's not a moral failing. It just is.

The problem is that *we've* built a world that isn't built for us.

Wandering the savanna 250,000 years ago, our earliest ancestors were not beholden to an endless horizon full of billboards or an infinite scroll of notifications. Instead, we evolved in a world with very real threats—dealing with many more things that wanted to eat us than we do today—and we developed behaviors that allowed us to quickly scan the environment and shift our attention to help us stay one step ahead. Some branches rustling or shadows shifting could indicate a predator around the bend, and immediately our eyes widen and our ears perk up to judge the threat.

As evidenced by the fact that you and I are still here, our ancient relatives were really good at not being eaten. These brains of ours worked! Our attention and memory filters did their job.

But today, we've invited that saber-toothed threat into our homes and pockets. Our devices cry out constantly, jolting our minds from one urgent thing to the next. And the pace is only quickening.

The Golden Age of Distraction

Every semester as I teach my undergraduates, I ask them to pull out their phones, tap over to the settings, and view their daily screen time totals. I then tell the class to shout out the biggest numbers. Here are some of their responses: "5 hours, 23 minutes," "6 hours, 14 minutes," "7 hours, 51 minutes."

Taken in the context of a twenty-four-hour day, these numbers are wild—but they aren't out of the ordinary. In the United States, 57 percent of adults spend five or more hours on their phones each day.[14] I'm right there in the mix myself, racking up an average of four hours and seven minutes during the week I wrote this.

If we extend our view to all media, from smartphones to computers, television, radio, books, newspapers, and maga-zines, Americans average over thirteen hours a day of having messaging blasted into our brains.[15] If you take away the time for sleeping and bathing, that's pretty much everything.

In this time, we see and receive thousands of images and messages, from friends and family, from organizations and groups, and, of course, from advertisers, all stewed together in our algorithmic feeds. With our phones and apps designed to be addictive, some marketers estimate that we scroll more than three hundred feet daily through our various feeds, a distance longer than the Statue of Liberty is tall. We cover so much ground on our phones alone that doctors have reported a new malady dubbed *smartphone finger*, a form of tendinitis from the constant flick, flick, flick.

The battle against information overload is not new, but it has reached new heights. In 1255, Dominican Vincent of Beauvais complained of "the multitude of books, the shortness of time and the slipperiness of memory."[16] And that was nearly two hundred years before the printing press led to an explosion of the written word. As the centuries marched on, newspapers, radio, and television took up more of that "shortness of time," and in the accelerating present era, it's been ever worsening.

We're struggling to stay afloat against this flood of information, installing ad blockers by the millions and unsubscribing en masse. We buy smartwatches to help clear notifications faster. These efforts don't matter, though, as the large and powerful forces pushing the other way are incentivized for more and more and more. We live in the golden age of distraction, and piercing through this noise is harder than ever.

In his book *Emotional Design*, designer Don Norman explains the crux of the problem with these distractive technologies. By using them, "you are doing a very special sort of activity, for you are a part of two different spaces, one where you are located physically, the other a mental space, the private location within your mind where you interact with the person on the other end of the conversation."[17]

This split consciousness, combined with this fire hose of information, creates a world unrecognizable to our great-grandparents, let alone our evolutionary forebears. We're busy, with less downtime than hunter-gatherers by some estimates, and we're distracted, receiving an average of one hundred twenty emails and fifty push notifications a day, and we're simply unable to keep up.[18]

The Default Is Indifference

It's not just you. The data shows that social media trends move faster today than even just a few years ago and that our interest in both the latest books and movies is more fleeting than it once was.[19] More and more comes at us each year. Behind each wave of stuff screaming for attention, there is another bigger one. In this age of abundance, the deluge never stops.

The vast majority of us, nearly three-quarters of the population, say there are too many ads. And the ones that hijack our attention the most, blaring autoplay video ads, are considered far and away the most annoying.[20] Whether by installing blockers or changing our habits to otherwise get around them, most of us do whatever we can to avoid advertising everywhere we can. Four US states even ban billboards.

The way we respond to this onslaught of annoyance is by tuning out. Our default is to ignore.

Banner blindness, a form of selective attention that blocks out these uninvited messages, has been documented in computer users for decades.[21] Our brains are so trained to ignore ads, and even things that look like ads, when we're using websites and apps that we instinctively know how to skip right by them even if we've never been to that page before. We literally don't see these messages, and we certainly don't receive them. The signal is lost in the noise.

This collective failure of communication results from our core, underlying, and all-too-obvious motivation: we just want to do what we want to do.

To put it bluntly, we don't care about things unless they matter to us. We love and care deeply about our friends and families, our sports teams and political parties, our hobbies and our faith. These and many other subjects do matter to us and command our attention. But when we don't immediately see that something aligns with our goals and desires, we move on to the next thing. And there are more of those next things than ever before.

Our brains created this mess, and they can get us out of it. As we've seen, before we even try to communicate, the deck is stacked against us. Our biology and psychology want us to tune the noise out, and the world we've created is so full of clutter and chaos that it's a miracle anything gets through at all.

We're bringing a Stone Age brain to a smartphone fight. It's not our fault when we lose.

But we can't just give in. We have important things to say, movements to build, and innovations to bring forth. Communication is too vital—to business, to our lives, to the grand project of society—to allow it to fail. It's the essence of our humanity, and to do it right we must acknowledge and embrace our human limitations. To do the work to cut through and be heard is our responsibility.

And as it turns out, there's a science behind how we can do just that.

What's Going On in Our Heads

A lot of details are at play every time we create or communicate. Here's a partial list of the ideas we discuss in our journey to understand how a message gets from sender to receiver:

- *Availability bias*—We are more likely to use ideas that are closer at hand.
- *Complexity bias*—We tend to look at situations, tasks, or issues as more complex than they actually are.
- *False-consensus effect*—We tend to overrate how much our opinions and choices are shared by everybody else.
- *Fluency heuristic*—We judge situations or ideas more favorably when they are easily perceived and understood.
- *Homophily*—We tend to associate with people who are similar to us.
- *Instrumentality heuristic*—We can sometimes prefer tasks that take more effort, but only when we're motivated in pursuit of a goal.
- *Overconfidence effect*—We have a tendency to overestimate our performance, knowledge, and ability, particularly in areas of limited experience.
- *Selective attention*—We have the ability to tunnel our attention into a specific task, ignoring other details around us.

2

The Case for Simplicity

Simple can be harder than complex: You have to work hard to get your thinking clean to make it simple. But it's worth it in the end because once you get there, you can move mountains.

—Steve Jobs

Over the course of a couple of weeks in March 2020, the world as we knew it screeched to a halt. The NBA abruptly shut down its season midway through a game. Cruise ships were ordered to immediately stop under a no-sail order. The New York City public school system, the nation's largest, closed its doors. A new virus, COVID-19, brought our modern life to a standstill.

But as our species began to take shelter and socially distance, our neighbors on this planet did the exact opposite.

Between doom and gloom posts on social media, the world saw images of dolphins swimming in Istanbul's normally chaotic Bosphorus strait, cougars prowling urban streets in Santiago, and coyotes crossing the Golden Gate Bridge in San Francisco. "Nature is healing" was a familiar refrain as we saw what a quieter, calmer world meant for the environment.

Almost overnight, urban noise levels fell to lows not seen since the middle of the last century. Less traffic on the roads and fewer planes in the sky sent our cities back to the soundscape of the 1950s. I remember cycling around an eerily silent Manhattan that spring—you could hear a pin drop.

This quiet helped many city dwellers sleep better, but it also allowed another inhabitant of our cities to thrive in new ways: songbirds. As it turns out, birds used this newfound peace to sing more complex, nuanced songs.[1] When the noise of modern life returned in the months that followed, researchers found that detail washed away. Birds sang louder and simpler songs to cut through the din.

Even our feathered friends know the truth about how communication works in our busy, noisier world. If you want to be heard, by other birds or other people, you need to simplify what you say. We have a leg up on these birds though—we can use the brains that got us into this mess to help get us out.

What Is Simplicity?

Let's go back to the definition of simplicity in communications that we introduced at the beginning of this book.

Simple: When a message is easily perceived, understood, and acted upon

In other words, simplicity is a function of what scientists call *fluency*.

We know this word already. We can be fluent in English, Spanish, or Mandarin. We can be fluent in chess or cooking, wine or woodworking. Where we are fluent, things are quick, easy, and smooth. The word itself stems from the Latin *fluens*, meaning "flowing"—which is just what it feels like.

When psychologists and neuroscientists talk about fluency, they are referring to a suite of experiences that we'll distill down to two major buckets, perceptual fluency and processing fluency:

- *Perceptual fluency*—How easily do we notice things?
- *Processing fluency*—How easily do we understand things?

An incredible body of evidence across a wide range of factors points to the same result: we are naturally biased toward things that are easier to perceive and process. When our experience with a message or concept is more fluent, we're more likely to believe it, trust it, prefer it, and choose it.

In a slightly absurd example of our behavior toward fluency, look to the fluctuations of the stock market. When companies go public, depending on the exchange, they choose a ticker symbol of up to four or five characters. Walmart is known as WMT, Tesla as TSLA, and McDonald's as MCD. In theory, these shorthand symbols should have no bearing on how the company performs. Leadership, market conditions, and technological breakthroughs power the growth (or decline) in a company's valuation, not just an irrelevant set of letters.

Well, not quite. Researchers Adam Alter and Daniel Oppenheimer took a list of nearly one thousand companies that went public over a period from 1990 to 2004[2] and divided them into two buckets: ones with symbols that you can pronounce and ones that you can't. Looking back on the historical performance of each group, they found that stocks with more easily pronounced ticker symbols regularly shot higher than the ones that were impossible to read. If you invested $1,000 dollars on the simpler, more readable stock symbols, and your friend invested the same amount spread over the unpronounceable ones, after the first day of trading you'd be ahead by $85. The effect diminishes after the post-IPO boom, but even years later, the positive effect still lingers.

When it becomes easier for investors to say and hold the name in their minds, they are more likely to remember and invest in it. Remembering GOOGL, DIS, and PEP is less mentally taxing than CMCSA, ACN, and VZ (Google's parent company Alphabet, Disney, and Pepsi, and Comcast, Accenture, and Verizon, respectively).

Our preference toward clearer, more easily pronounceable names extends beyond stocks and into the boardroom itself. Even when accounting for length, uniqueness, and ethnicity, we regularly judge people with more pronounceable names more positively. Studies show that we're more likely to vote for candidates with easier names, that lawyers with simpler-to-say names advance further in their careers, and that overall, the easily verbalized are just generally more liked—fairly or not.[3]

Simpler names are just the tip of the iceberg when it comes to our fluency bias. Nearly everywhere we look, fluency comes out ahead:

+ Options printed in easier-to-read typefaces are more likely to be purchased than ones displayed in blurry, cramped, or otherwise challenging text.
+ Images shown against a higher-contrast background are rated as prettier than ones presented against muddied, low-contrast backgrounds.[4]
+ Clean speech, without "uhs" and "ums," rates as more trustworthy than disjointed messages.
+ Visitors spend more time and more money on websites that load faster.
+ Even rhyming sentences are judged as truer than non-rhyming ones.

In our lived experience, this reality is intuitive. We agonize over having to follow unwieldy instructions to file our taxes, but we relish the opportunity to dive into a page-turning novel. Amazon and other e-commerce companies ruthlessly stripped out friction in the pursuit of a fluent, easy, one-click checkout experience that has run up our credit card bills. Easy things inspire positive feelings and action, and difficult things inspire the opposite.

Fluency is like a well-oiled hinge on the door to our minds. When opening that door is easy, we're more likely to let messages in. When the hinge is rusty, the locks are confusing, and it takes more work to pry the door open, we're less likely to use it.

Designing Simplicity

If we want to achieve fluent simplicity in our communications, how do we do that? Design.

Simply defined, *design* means to create with purpose. Design is a business function, not an art function.

If it isn't obvious by now, this book is not about poetry and paintings but instead dollars and cents. The world has plenty of room for sprawling, beautiful, intricate complexity in our creative pursuits, and indeed, this floating rock would be a pretty dreary place if we didn't have them. If you're creating art, follow your muse, not this book.

But when you are communicating with a purpose to inform or persuade, your message needs to be designed. Design has a *goal*.

Design comes in lots of shapes. I spent a decade running a marketing agency that designed all sorts of things. We designed mobile apps to help schools communicate with parents, websites that helped tourists plan their visits to famous landmarks, and brand identities that helped companies bring their products to market. I have friends who have designed buildings and bridges and others who have created products and the packages they come in. Some are flashy fashion designers or behind-the-scenes information architects. Wherever something, tangible or intangible, needs to be arranged to get a job done, there are designers.

But we often fail to remember that the way we communicate is one of those things. We see the results of designing interfaces and advertisements, but we think of the words and meaning as something separate, something that doesn't abide by the same laws of nature as everything else. The most effective communicators see messages as something that can, and must, be designed.

Designers deal with constraints. So far, we've taken stock of our own limitations and the environment we're in that makes it so hard for us to communicate.

Designers deal with consequences. We'll explore the perils of complicated, bloated, and unclear messages and see why they fail us so frequently.

And now, we're making the case for what does work—indeed, the only strategy that works: simplicity.

When we look at simplicity through the lens of design, looking at users and constraints and consequences, we discover five principles that all these messages share. Operating on each of them helps us unlock the benefits of fluency and become more effective communicators. Operating on all of them together helps us create the real magic.

Beneficial

Simple messages prioritize the receiver. They focus on the receiver's goals, needs, and desires. What's in it for them? How does your message help them?

Every exchange involves two parties—but they are not equal. Just as the sender of a letter must pay the postage, the sender of a message is responsible for carrying the real and figurative cost of communication. Why? The sender wants those purchases, votes, or donations, and the receiver is perfectly happy without doing any of that.

Focused

Simple messages cut out all the stuff that doesn't matter. Everything is there to get the point across, and anything else that's a distraction is vigorously stripped away. Empty platitudes, useless fluff, anything that isn't a necessary component of your story is another place to lose the receiver. You have only a small window to be heard, so don't waste it.

Design is not the same thing as decoration. Decoration is adding ornamentation to "pretty things up." When we add chrome fenders to our car or put on a piece of sparkling jewelry, that's decoration. Nothing is wrong with that, but decoration is art—and design is business, and it requires focus.

Salient

Simple messages stand out. Psychologists and neuroscientists use the term *salience* to describe how much things stick out from the crowd and rise to our attention. In a noisy world, you need to be conspicuously distinct to have any hope of being noticed. The brain readily adapts to repeated stimuli, blurring muddy sameness into the background, and we are predisposed to things that don't.

Contrast can be achieved in many ways: in physical appearance, tone of voice, size or length, volume, style, or placement or by pushing and pulling a host of other attributes. It all comes down to being different. Salient messages zig when others zag. Simple stands out, complicated blends in.

Empathetic

Simple messages show understanding of the receiver. Empathetic messages speak the receiver's language and exhibit insight into their reality. They don't require specialized lingo, a degree's worth of prior knowledge, or a dictionary full of esoteric words.

As marketer and author Michael Ventura says in his book *Applied Empathy*, "Empathy lets us see the world from other points of view and helps us form insights that can lead us to new and better ways of thinking, being, and doing."[5] Empathetic communicators put themselves in the shoes of their audience, and unlock greater understanding and connection in the process.

Minimal

Simple messages contain everything they need but only what they need. They require the fewest number of dependencies— and thus have the fewest possible points of failure.

While minimal generally correlates with short length, that doesn't mean shortness is the goal. Instead, the attribute that minimal measures is friction. More stuff means more friction and more work. Less friction means greater fluency.

The Simplicity Edge

But why is all of that so important? If our nature pushes us one way, why should we do the hard work to push back in the other direction? Because we're a lot like those songbirds from the beginning of the chapter. We don't have the luxury of perfect conditions, but we still need to communicate in this imperfect environment. Simplicity is our path forward.

Simplicity Is Tested

Simplicity is not new. Far from it. Indeed, this idea has been tested in every arena in every generation.

Most notably, fourteenth-century Franciscan friar William of Occam is popularly remembered for his namesake "razor," or rule of thumb: simpler explanations are more likely to be correct. Across science, medicine, and history, when we look for explanations for what happens around us, we continually see that the right answer is the simplest one, the one with the fewest assumptions and lowest number of hoops to jump through. More than a millennium before Occam, Aristotle is quoted as saying, "Nature operates in the shortest way possible."[6]

At the turn of the seventeenth century, Shakespeare wrote in *Hamlet* that "brevity is the soul of wit," and later in that century, Quakers developed their "testimony of simplicity" as a guiding principle in their faith. In the twentieth century, the United States Navy popularized the KISS principle, short for "Keep it simple, stupid." This blunt imperative has been used to develop everything from fighter planes to Disney movies and has driven both programmers and politicians in their craft.

Today, in our accelerating cultural moment, we see calls to simplicity all around us. Marie Kondo's simplicity-driven book *The Life-Changing Magic of Tidying Up* was such a smash hit that it inspired not only a Netflix show (so popular that some Goodwill stores saw donations spike by as much as 66 percent[7]) but also a series of bestselling parody books. And right there with Kondo on the top of streaming and bestseller charts are other influencers and authors reframing the austere tenets of stoicism. Meditation apps that help us block out the noise of this world are routinely at the top of download lists, and the makers of the phones that those apps run on have rolled out tools to help us cut down on their own distracting nature. After a pandemic that forced us to face our clutter inside, interior designers now say that "minimalism is in," and brands have been stripping away ornament and complexity in favor of more straightforward aesthetics.

In our modern consumer landscape, elegantly simple Apple products imagined and designed by Steve Jobs and Jony Ive have not only made billions of dollars for the world's largest corporation but have also inspired thousands of creators across countless industries. Before any of that, though, Dieter Rams inspired Jobs and Ive. As the creative force behind the German consumer products brand Braun, Rams is one of the most influential figures in the history of design—and a thoughtful advocate of simplicity. His philosophy brings together all these centuries of combined human experience: "Good design is as little design as possible. Less, but better because it concentrates on the essential aspects, and the products are not burdened with nonessentials. Back to purity, back to simplicity."[8]

In every era, when faced with challenges and uncertainty, we return to that same principle. What wins, what we want, and what moves us is just that: less, but better.

Simplicity Is Kind

Since the movie *Toy Story*, Pixar has been pumping out hit after hit. It has been commercially successful, critically acclaimed, and culturally adored. Its style has been imitated, and the company has been put under a microscope to help distill its secret to success. In 2012, Emma Coats, a story-board artist at the studio, shared a list of rules for storytelling that she picked up from her world-class collaborators, one being "You gotta keep in mind what's interesting to you as an audience, not what's fun to do as a writer."[9]

Simplicity, by being focused on the receiver, is a form of kindness. Valuing other people's time and desires is generous. Putting yourself in their shoes is empathetic. But kindness and niceness are not the same thing. Niceness is surface level: pleasing, polite, and conflict-avoidant. Kindness goes much deeper; being kind means you actually care about others and their well-being.

Complicated messages can be full of niceties but not kind to the receiver's limited time and attention. And bad news, delivered with respect and honesty, is kinder than mealy-mouthed avoidance.

In New York City, former mayor Ed Koch embodied the blunt to-the-point manner that shapes my hometown's repu-tation around the world. During his first term, his adminis-tration installed the most straightforward No Parking signs you'll ever see: "Don't even THINK of parking here."[10] The sign was so popular that they rolled it out in Chinese, Yiddish, and other languages throughout the city—and today still sell copies of it to collectors. It even spawned a spin-off, "No

Parking, No Standing, No Stopping, No Kidding." When they were removed in favor of more byzantine signage after his tenure, New Yorkers bristled, some claiming that the new signs "intentionally make it confusing so they can write a lot of tickets" as shown in figure 2.1.[11]

That simple sign might not be very nice, but it's certainly kind.

Simplicity Is Efficient

Advertising is an industry of constraints. Your commercial must be exactly thirty seconds to air. Your full-page ad in *Time* magazine must be exactly 7.875 inches wide and 10.5 inches tall to run.[12] For generations, anybody posting a job opening or even looking for love would pay by the word or "column inch" to get their message seen in the local newspaper.

Even today, in a world where Meta, Google, and Amazon have eaten a full half of the entire advertising industry,

Figure 2.1. If you can choose only one,
it's better to be kind than nice.

constraints are everywhere.[13] A search ad on Google tops out at a puny thirty characters for a headline and ninety characters for a description. That's so short that the last sentence just now that explained the length is itself too long to be used as an ad. Pixels and keystrokes are free, but eyeballs and attention are expensive.

Simplicity, by its nature, is efficient. Simplicity requires that we strip away the excess and leave only what works. When we do that, we cut out the costs associated with all that fluff and ultimately get the most bang for our buck.

A century ago, John Wanamaker, a Philadelphia retailer and early marketing pioneer, complained, "Half the money I spend on advertising is wasted, and the trouble is I don't know which half."[14] I have a hunch about the answer—it's probably the half that didn't need to be there in the first place. When we pay for advertising that is self-serving, complicated, and not squarely focused on the customer and their needs, then we're flushing money down the toilet.

Simplicity Is Effective

Finally, all of this is for nothing if simple doesn't work. Good thing it does.

Brand strategy and design firm Siegel+Gale has been tracking the state of simplicity in marketing for the past ten years, surveying thousands of consumers worldwide and evaluating hundreds of brands across every major industry.[15] Every year, it sees more and more of the same results. Not only do the simplest brands outperform the competition, but people are both willing to pay more for them and more likely to recommend them:

+ 76 percent of consumers are more likely to recommend a simpler brand.
+ 57 percent of consumers are willing to pay more for a simpler brand.
+ Companies have left $402 billion on the table by failing to get simple.

The most memorable ads and slogans of all time are clear, straightforward, and focus on the receiver:

+ Nike's direct "Just Do It" campaign allowed it to multiply its business more than ten times in its first ten years running.
+ When FedEx reframed its offer as "When it absolutely, positively has to be there overnight," it quickly reached $1 billion in revenue and went on to become the largest cargo airline in the world.
+ Burger King contrasted its flexibility against its rival's stiffness with "Have it your way," a message so potent they've come back to it in campaigns over and over again.

Simple messages can change our society. In 1998, more than 20 percent of American high school students smoked cigarettes daily. Tobacco use for anybody invites a host of health problems, but children and teens are particularly susceptible to developing severe addictions, stunting their lung development, and developing dangerous respiratory illnesses.[16] It's a serious epidemic that has been made worse by a massive investment by tobacco companies to paper over concerns.

In response, Florida's public health authorities launched an education campaign designed to fight back against tobacco advertising and disinformation. The name, and aim, were blunt: "truth." Later being incorporated into the Truth Initiative and going nationwide, truth's most recognizable PSA series involved stunts outside of tobacco company offices. In one, trucks pull up and dump 1,200 "body bags" on the sidewalk, and in another, 1,200 numbered volunteers suddenly collapse in the street. The salient message, shouted clearly to the executives up above and viewers at home, was "Tobacco kills 1,200 people a day. Ever think about taking a day off?"

Tobacco giant Philip Morris was actually required to also make anti-smoking PSAs that aired around the same time. *They weren't great.* The campaign, under the banner "Think. Don't Smoke," involved some confusing narratives, bad acting, and half-hearted execution.

Studies of these campaigns in the years since have proven two things. First, the truth campaign worked, consistently increasing anti-smoking attitudes in teens. Second, the Philip Morris campaign wasn't just ineffective but counterproductive: teens exposed to the clunky ads ended up *more* likely to be interested in smoking. Thankfully, "truth" prevailed, and today, teen cigarette use is down to just 4.6 percent.[17] And with the new challenge of teen vaping, truth has since been relaunched to help finish the job.

Simplicity isn't just window dressing, it's an entirely different way of thinking about how we communicate with each other. If we step back, design, and communicate with intention, we can move mountains.

But it's not so easy. We must first face a familiar foe.

3

The Crime of Complicated

Clutter and confusion are failures of design,
not attributes of information.

—Edward Tufte

In the winter of 1944, the world was on fire.

At the same time as Allied forces were engaged in a shooting war thousands of miles away, back home, the American war apparatus was working around the clock to find every way to gain the upper hand. In the offices of what would later become the CIA (at the time, the Office of Strategic Services), one team was developing a particularly unique way to do just that, a guide for spies in enemy territory called the *Simple Sabotage Field Manual.*

The mission of this highly classified publication was to "characterize simple sabotage, to outline its possible effects, and to present suggestions for inciting and executing it." Pages and pages detail how to gum up factories, derail transportation networks, and interrupt power supplies. Spies or trusted allies are instructed to "change signposts at intersections and forks" and to "put several pinches of sawdust or hard grain, such as rice or wheat, into the fuel tank of a gasoline engine."[1]

But right there, among the devious lists of ways to ruin the enemy's economy, are a set of instructions for ruining organizations:

> Make "speeches." Talk as frequently as possible and at great length. Illustrate your "points" by long anecdotes and accounts of personal experiences. Never hesitate to make a few appropriate "patriotic" comments. . . .
>
> Bring up irrelevant issues as frequently as possible. . . .
>
> When training new workers, give incomplete or misleading instructions. . . .
>
> Give lengthy and incomprehensible explanations when questioned.

In pursuit of making the enemy less productive and effective, to lower their morale and gain the upper hand, spies were taught to *complicate* matters. Does any of this sound familiar in our own lives?

If you've ever been on a team at work, in school, or in your community, you likely know (and have suffered from) somebody who has embodied all these conspiratorial traits—intentionally or not. Maybe we've even been the culprit ourselves.

When we're bad communicators and we complicate and jumble our message, we're sabotaging ourselves in the same way that spies are taught to sabotage the enemy. This is how our communication fails.

Complicated versus Complex

Before we go on, let's establish a fundamental distinction between two words that, on their face, seem to have the same definition: *complicated* and *complex*. One of them is a benign state, and the other is an act of sabotage (see figure 3.1).

International diplomacy is complex. The bad check-in instructions you got from your Airbnb host are complicated.

A computer chip is complex. Getting your printer to actually work is complicated.

Corporate mergers are complex. The dense memo about your office's new PTO policy is complicated.

Lots of systems, objects, and actions in this world are complex. Complexity is when something has a lot of parts, often interconnected in an intricate and detailed fashion. The human eye is complex. Theoretical physics is complex. Machine learning is complex. Whether in nature or artificially

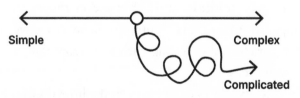

Figure 3.1. Complicated is unnecessary complexity.

made, many of the most miraculous things in the universe are inherently complex.

Your message is not one of those.

Complicated is when something is complex but it could be simple. We *complicate* as a verb. Complicated is when things are too long, too cumbersome, and too confusing. Complicated causes friction because complicated is unfinished. Complicated things work, but they take work. You really don't want your message to take work.

We frequently put up with complexity because lots of complex goals are worth it. Playing the piano is complex, but some people put in years of practice because it does something for them—it's worthwhile.

People read *War and Peace* every day because they want to experience great literature. Your ad for a new shampoo or your annual shareholder report doesn't meet this bar. It shouldn't be complicated.

We Default to More—It's the Easy Route

The problem is, we are programmed to complicate and it's our greatest weakness when seeking to connect.

We are subject to a complexity bias, by which we are predisposed to push ideas toward that end of the spectrum—to complicate them. This complexity is so attractive to us because, paradoxically, dealing with a complex task is easier than a simple one.

Complexity allows us to focus on the little things, to distract ourselves in the nuance of details instead of dealing with one large truth. When a challenge has lots of little parts, we have lots of places to put our attention. When we have only one big thing for us to deal with, we can't help but notice it.

We prefer to noodle around with the formatting of our document instead of critically reevaluating our big idea. We choose to dig into reviews to find the best desk chair to alleviate our back pain instead of questioning our choice to spend eight hours a day sitting in one. We tinker around the edges instead of getting to the point. As described in an article on *Farnam Street*, "Of the fight-or-flight responses, complexity bias is the flight response. It is a means of turning away from a problem or concept and labeling it as too confusing. If you think something is harder than it is, you surrender your responsibility to understand it."[2]

Our brains push us down this path of unintuitive least resistance in a number of ways. In 1989, the University of California's Hilary Farris and Russell Revlin ran a study where participants were asked to determine the fundamental pattern between sets of numbers like those shown in figure 3.2.[3] While the actual relationship was simple—they were just presented in ascending order—most participants saw right past that and instead developed complicated arithmetic to explain their relationship. We are built to ignore the simple route right in front of us.

Leidy Klotz, in his book *Subtract*, outlines further research done by him and his colleagues on this same additive bias.[4] In one experiment, they presented students with Lego structures, asking them to make changes to the construction to allow it to balance. Adding each block would cost the subject ten cents, and the goal was to accomplish this while spending the least. The most rational solution would be to remove a

Figure 3.2. What pattern do you see in this number sequence?

single block, but less than half of the participants chose to do that. Instead, they were more likely to add a handful of bricks to prop up the structure.

The same preference for more emerged when the research team asked subjects to alter patterns of colored tiles on a screen, change a vacation itinerary, remodel a minigolf course, adjust a soup recipe, compose a musical tune, or improve a piece of writing. Everywhere they looked, they found that our brains pushed us to add first, ignoring even the possibility of simplification.

When we rise to the conscious level, we also see that our incentives push toward complexity and addition. Adding a new page to the employee handbook, putting another paragraph on our home page, or writing another memo leaves evidence of our work and effort. Subtraction, by simplifying or omitting those same things, leaves a lot less for us to point to. Absence offers little proof.

All our biological and sociological preferences for more can be explained by the fact that our species has lived most of our existence in a world of great scarcity and uncertainty. We didn't know when the next mammoth was coming our way, we didn't know if the next harvest would be fruitful, and we didn't know if our village would be invaded by the tribe across the river. We needed to save and accumulate and build our stockpiles to protect against the unknown. Addition was in our best interest. It helped us survive in this uneven and dangerous world.

And while today the future is still unknown, in the past century we've made it a whole lot more knowable and predictable—and abundant.

The most scarce resource these days, as we learned in chapter 1, is our time and attention. Coping with the abundance of forces competing for both is our defining challenge as citizens of the twenty-first century. We live in a different moment than any other time in our history. And this is why we cannot allow ourselves to become victims of the complicated.

The Three Sins of Complicated

In our case, we have three counts against the accused. First, complicated messages are selfish, being used as a way to prioritize the sender—and to hide malfeasance. Second, they are cowardly, allowing senders to hide within and behind them. And finally, they are dangerous, both to our bottom line and to our very lives. Let's look at each sin in order.

Selfish

When we fall back into the crutch of fluffy, easy complication, we're being selfish. We're prioritizing our comfort and ease over that of the receiver. Complicated messages are unsympathetic toward the other party and assume the receiver both can and wants to invest in decoding what you mean.

In the best case, this clutter results in a missed opportunity. Maybe you wasted a few dollars on ads that didn't perform. But in darker cases, this selfishness makes us all worse off.

We can see how complicated communication is used against us every day—maybe even right now as you're reading this. Over the course of an average day, we use dozens of online services, from scrolling through TikTok and Instagram in our Uber to flipping between Slack, Dropbox, and Zoom once we get to work. To use each of these platforms, we have to sign off on a Terms of Service agreement, usually hidden away behind a checkbox and some fine print when we're first setting up our accounts. Though we all breeze past them, a lot of important information is squirreled away in these documents, including many things we probably wouldn't be thrilled with. Here are just a few of the many shady conditions to be found in user agreements:

- Facebook can use you in ads shown to others.
- YouTube is granted access to view your browser history.
- Pinterest can read your private messages.[5]

If you've ever popped open one of these agreements to scan through it, you'll see that they are long—*really* long.[6] In a survey of these major platforms, Instagram's 2,451-word agreement is the shortest. Tinder clocks in at 6,215 words, Spotify at 8,600 words, and Microsoft tops the list with a bewildering 15,260-word user agreement. It would take more than an hour to read the entire Microsoft document alone, a long wait before you get to boot up Word. If you wanted to read all the contracts you sign off on to live a digital life, you'd need to carve out approximately 250 hours. Better bring extra highlighters.

It's not just the length that is hiding all this sneaky business but also the density of the writing. When analyzed for readability, most of these agreements are rated at a college-level difficulty—meanwhile, the median reading comprehension level in the United States is closer to a sixth-grade level. These documents that all of us are forced to agree to are hidden, long, and difficult to read, and make us give up our rights and privacy in the process. The purpose of all these complications is purely selfish, purely to provide protection and profit to the companies producing them.

As George Orwell wrote, "A mass of Latin words falls upon the facts like soft snow, blurring the outline and covering up all the details. The great enemy of clear language is insincerity."[7] Long, confusing, and fluff-filled messages are selfish because they put the sender first, wasting the receiver's precious time and attention in the process.

Cowardly

We complicate when we are afraid. We complicate when we don't know our stuff and want to hide behind a wall of words. We complicate when we are worried that we're going to be found out for the frauds that we secretly think we are.

Making it through a tough client meeting by filibustering until the clock runs out is easier than admitting that you screwed up or you don't know. We may be tempted to throw out some big words, unrelated statistics or references, or misleading framing to weasel out of a jam. I know this personally. I've been in plenty of client meetings where we have to share some bad news or face questioning we'd rather deflect. It can seem that as long as you spit out enough syllables, the other side will feel like they got an answer even if they didn't.

More complicated messaging increases ambiguity, allowing the receiver to hear whatever they want to hear. In politics, candidates are notorious for making ambiguous statements, which you'll see on yard signs across America every election season: broad platitudes of freedom and family, community and respect. This fuzziness helps candidates avoid taking hard stances on divisive issues, and who can blame them? Strategic ambiguity gives the voter, the receiver in this instance, a chance to see in the message something that might resonate with their already held beliefs. But that type of language is just a mirror, not a message. It doesn't communicate, inform, or persuade.

Those jargon-filled monologues and reports that we give when our backs are against the wall are also a manifestation of our own insecurities. If we don't know our stuff, or if we're worried that we're not smart enough or capable enough, we can use complicated language to compensate for our shortcomings. We think that if we use the right buzzwords and acronyms, maybe we can fool the audience into thinking we know what we're talking about.

We see "lower status" groups often compensate for this perceived inadequacy by using more jargon than "higher status" ones. In a 2020 study of academic papers, researchers found that authors from schools further down the popular *US News and World Reports* university rankings were more likely to use unnecessarily complex language and acronyms than ones from more prestigious universities.[8] Researchers have seen the same pattern when undergrads interact with MBA students and when lawyers from low- and high-power law firms engage with each other. Even smaller airports are more likely to describe themselves as "international" than larger airports. When we're afraid of not measuring up, we put on the stage dressing of more.

This type of needlessly complicated language has stunted our search for knowledge and truth and compromised our ability to trust experts and leaders, which carries a price we all pay in our age of "alternative facts." Scientific literature is already notoriously some of the densest and most indecipherable writing out there, and the overlap in the Venn diagram of trustworthy scientists and great communicators is a vanishingly small sliver.

While researching for this book, I read hundreds of studies and papers, so I know firsthand how dense and unreadable some of this stuff is. Sometimes it feels like the authors want to keep their ideas secret. And they apparently have succeeded in this accidental goal: as many as 50 percent of papers are never read by anybody but their authors and editors.[9]

In 1996, physics professor Alan Sokal tested how much anybody actually reads these studies by submitting an article to a cultural studies journal. Except, his paper wasn't well researched or intelligent—it was jargon-filled gibberish titled "Transgressing the Boundaries: Toward a Transformative Hermeneutics of Quantum Gravity." The journal published it. In the years since, dozens and dozens of other fake articles have gotten through the publishing process—including one

in 2020 that linked the COVID-19 pandemic to human consumption of the Pokémon Zubat.[10]

These authors largely aimed to call out predatory pseudo-
academic journals, but in doing so they also proved that
language can be used to mask true meaning. As we begin to
grapple with the future of generative artificial intelligence producing endless reams of content, the challenge of deciphering
meaning from language will only get harder.

The "academese" that these prank studies bathed themselves in to deceive journal publishers is not the only dialect
that has sprung up across industries to build walls around what
they really mean. The Federal Reserve engages in ambiguous
"Fedspeak" to obscure its intentions. Lawyers charge top dollar to speak in "legalese," bureaucrats deal in "officialese,"
and skyscrapers are filled with suits speaking "corporatese."
"Psychobabble" and "technobabble" frequently make about
as much sense as a baby's babbling. Oftentimes the words
themselves don't matter—they just need to fill in the blank
with something that sounds right. To that end, science fiction
screenwriters have even written the phrase "tech the tech" in the
first drafts of their scripts, having science consultants come in
later to fill in the blanks with some plausible set of syllables.[11]

Plausible—that's the secret of complication. Complicated
gives us a plausible way out of our responsibility to ourselves
and our audience.

Dangerous

On the brisk morning of January 16, 2003, the fuse was
lit on 3.8 million pounds of rocket fuel. Attached to these

enormous engines, the space shuttle *Columbia* slowly heaved, then quickly climbed toward the heavens.

After eighty-one of those roaring seconds, a two-foot-wide chunk of insulation foam shook off the side of the left booster, crashing into the shuttle's wing on its way down. Though nobody noticed it at the time, this piece of debris, moving at approximately five hundred miles per hour, chipped away at the protective tiles that would allow the shuttle to safely withstand the intense heat of reentry.

After *Columbia* settled into orbit, NASA conducted its routine review of the launch. Analysts spotted the falling debris and fed it up the chain of command, and soon an ad hoc Debris Assessment Team was assembled to make sure the craft, and most importantly the seven crew members, were safe.

As the crew worked diligently on their two-week mission, the analysts on the ground quickly assessed the data. Anything smacking into the side of a rocket ship is obviously troublesome, but this dilemma wasn't new to the shuttle program. In fact, on the first ever shuttle flight in 1981, also with *Columbia*, a similar foam strike against the heat shield occurred. Since then, out of the seventy-nine missions with available imagery, foam hitting the spacecraft can be seen in sixty-five of them. This event therefore wasn't rare by any means, but NASA still wanted to look into it. Business as usual.

Engineers from Boeing, one of NASA's partners, prepared multiple reports totaling twenty-eight PowerPoint slides.[12] But buried deep on the fourteenth line of the sixth page of the second report was the point that should have set this incident apart from the others—but didn't: "Flight condition is significantly outside of test database. Volume of ramp is 1920cu in vs 3 cu in for test" (see figure 3.3).

What on earth does that mean? These stiff, jargon-filled lines basically said this: while they have previously tested debris impacts of three inches, the piece of foam that hit *Columbia*'s wing was actually *640 times larger*.

Now, not many things don't matter when they are off by 64,000 percent, especially in space. This warning should have been shouted from the rooftops but was instead clouded with confusing language and hidden deep inside a dry report. The word *significantly* in this bullet was the fifth time it appeared

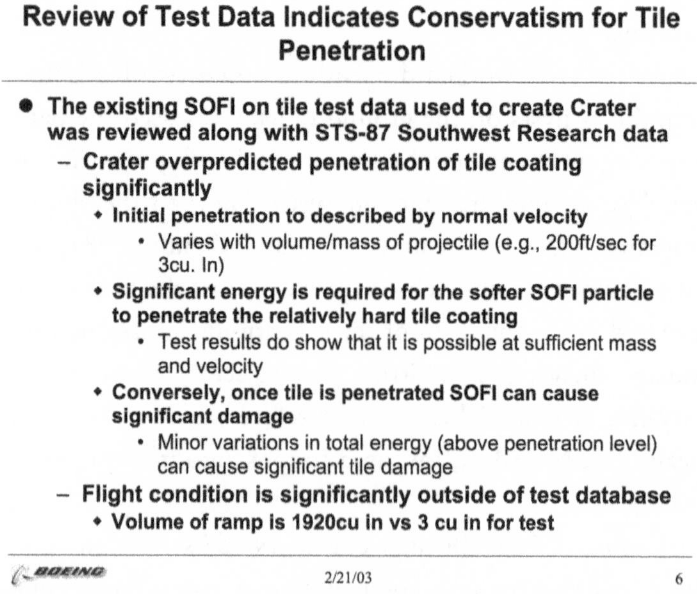

Review of Test Data Indicates Conservatism for Tile Penetration

- **The existing SOFI on tile test data used to create Crater was reviewed along with STS-87 Southwest Research data**
  - **Crater overpredicted penetration of tile coating significantly**
    - **Initial penetration to described by normal velocity**
      - Varies with volume/mass of projectile (e.g., 200ft/sec for 3cu. In)
    - **Significant energy is required for the softer SOFI particle to penetrate the relatively hard tile coating**
      - Test results do show that it is possible at sufficient mass and velocity
    - **Conversely, once tile is penetrated SOFI can cause significant damage**
      - Minor variations in total energy (above penetration level) can cause significant tile damage
  - **Flight condition is significantly outside of test database**
    - **Volume of ramp is 1920cu in vs 3 cu in for test**

Figure 3.3. The key slide from the Debris Assessment Team. What's the important message here?

on that same slide, each with a different implied meaning. The slide's headline is both dense and contradicted by the content of the slide itself. And the author uses four levels of bullet points, along with three different formats of the same measurement, before getting to the most critical point.

The report didn't say why this data was important. It didn't make the information salient and unmissable. It didn't use clear, easy-to-understand language. The message didn't communicate.

The message should have raised alarms or at least questions. Instead of the borderline-incomprehensible title of "Review of Test Data Indicates Conservatism for Tile Penetration," the slide should have read "Debris Impact Hundreds of Times Larger Than Test Data, Danger Unknown."

Unfortunately, that's not what happened. The irrelevant data from the much smaller test was then used to justify other conclusions, and mission command decided to continue with the flight as planned.

As decision-makers would have known if they heard this warning, the large piece of foam that hit *Columbia*'s wing left a sixteen-inch gash in the orbiter's heat shield—compromising the craft's protection from the intense three-thousand-degree heat of reentry.

On February 1, at 1:44 p.m., the shuttle began its journey back to Earth, descending rapidly from four hundred thousand feet. A few moments later, sensors detected abnormal stress on the left wing. Then sensors in the left wheel noticed a rise in temperature. As the craft flew over California, observers could see debris flying off the shuttle, which was now brightly glowing from the stress and heat. Finally, at

1:59 p.m., mission control lost contact with *Columbia*, which disintegrated in the blue afternoon sky high above Texas. All seven astronauts on board tragically perished.

Lives were lost because of a failure to communicate a vital message clearly, and American space flight was grounded for nearly two years. This disaster was the beginning of the end for the Space Shuttle program, which flew its final flight in 2011. Communication errors were also partly to blame for the program's other fatal disaster, the 1986 *Challenger* explosion.

Closer to home, 70 percent of commercial aviation incidents can be traced back to miscommunication. And four out of five medical errors are a result of miscommunication.[13] Businesses lose $400 billion every year to bad writing. Investor Charlie Munger once said, "Where you have complexity, by nature you can have fraud and mistakes." Not being heard isn't a victimless crime.[14]

Another iconic business leader from the last century, GE's Jack Welch, was well-known for his distaste of cluttered thinking and communication. In an interview at the height of his powers, he lamented, "Insecure managers create complexity. Frightened, nervous managers use thick, convoluted planning books and busy slides filled with everything they've known since childhood."[15] Later in that discussion, he reaches the same conclusion as shown in the study above: "You can't believe how hard it is for people to be simple, how much they fear being simple. They worry that if they're simple, people will think they're simpleminded. In reality, of course, it's just the reverse. Clear, tough-minded people are the most simple."

Cowering in the complicated can cost those executives and their investors lots of money. When you compare more readable to less readable corporate financial disclosures, the lousy, dense ones are correlated to lower firm valuations. All else being equal, dropping in readability one standard deviation from the average can ding values by 2.5 percent—a plague totaling billions across the economy.[16]

Across every metric, not being heard hurts us.

Getting Simple

A simple message, when executed properly, is dumbfounding. It's inescapable. Unarguable. It makes you go, "Well, yeah." It offers no room to hide. It's refreshing. Your brain sparkles when you understand something that clearly.

When we look to psychology and biology, history and culture, economics and business, we see that simplicity is the key that unlocks our full ability to connect and truly reach others. In an age of disconnected connection, it's the most valuable thing we can do.

But it's not that easy. We're standing in our own way, sabotaging ourselves individually and collectively. As we've just seen, our bias toward complication stops us from connecting and hurts us all in the process. This is the villain in our story.

The second half of this book helps us slay this dragon. In it, we'll explore the five principles of simplicity and then show proven methods to bring each to bear in our own pursuit of authentic, effective, and worthwhile communication. We'll start with the single most influential mindset shift you can make.

PART 2

How
to
Get
Simple

4

Beneficial:
The Hole, Not the Drill

Eh, what's in it for me to be "vewy, vewy quiet"?

—Bugs Bunny

Beep. Beep. Beep.

This was the note that an NBC radio announcer called the "sound that forevermore separates the old from the new."[1] It was coming from a metallic beach ball hurtling through space. It was the sound of Sputnik—and it was the sound of defeat.

The United States struggled early in the space race, starting its losing streak when the Soviet Union launched that first satellite in 1957 and falling behind yet again when cosmonaut Yuri Gagarin became the first human in space in 1961.

Determined to catch up, John F. Kennedy sent an urgent memo just days after Gagarin returned to Earth. He asked his team for a solution: "Do we have a chance of beating the Soviets by putting a laboratory in space, or by a trip around the moon, or by a rocket to go to the moon and back with a man. Is there any other space program which promises dramatic results in which we could win?"

With some deliberation, the administration selected the most ambitious goal: landing a man on the moon. But beyond figuring out all the rocket science, it faced another problem—a lack of political will. In a Gallup poll that spring, 58 percent of Americans said they wouldn't want to shoulder the massive budget required for this endeavor.[2]

After Kennedy received a tepid response when he initially unveiled this project to Congress, his plan was in trouble. Would this embattled leader, fresh off a razor-thin election and an embarrassing fiasco at the Bay of Pigs, be able to sell this idea to the American people?

The following year, he tried making his case again. This time, Kennedy reintroduced this literal moonshot in front of a *slightly* larger crowd of approximately thirty-five thousand, at Rice University.[3] In this now-famous address, the president poetically outlined our nation's spirit of discovery and exploration, talked of the historic moment, and, most importantly, explained why it mattered:

> We set sail on this new sea because there is new knowledge to be gained, and new rights to be won, and they must be won and used for the progress of all people. For space science, like nuclear science and all technology, has

no conscience of its own. Whether it will become a force for good or ill depends on man, and only if the United States occupies a position of pre-eminence can we help decide whether this new ocean will be a sea of peace or a new terrifying theater of war. . . .

But why, some say, the moon? Why choose this as our goal? And they may well ask why climb the highest mountain? Why, thirty-five years ago, fly the Atlantic? . . .

We choose to go to the moon. We choose to go to the moon in this decade and do the other things, not because they are easy, but because they are hard, because that goal will serve to organize and measure the best of our energies and skills, because that challenge is one that we are willing to accept, one we are unwilling to postpone, and one which we intend to win, and the others, too.

Something unique about this speech makes it so effective as rhetoric and as, essentially, a sales pitch. Elsewhere in his address, Kennedy spoke about rocket engines, metal alloys, and guidance systems, and he also mentioned the dollars and cents of salaries and facility costs. But that's not the part we remember. Instead, the part that stirred the hearts of our nation was about something else, the benefits—the reason why.

What's the benefit of going to the moon? For one, we will gain "new knowledge," claim "new rights," and make science a "force for good." This project will "organize and measure the best of our energies and skills." But most of all, landing on the moon would mean we would "win." At a time when the world was a global chess match of us versus them, no call to action was more stirring than the promise of victory.

The message worked, and he had a deal. Over the next few years, the United States would commit over $25 billion toward the Apollo program, a total that in today's dollars would amount to more than $160 billion—one of the most expensive projects ever undertaken by anybody, anywhere, ever. On July 20, 1969, all that money, motivation, and engineering genius paid off as Neil Armstrong and Buzz Aldrin became the first humans to set foot on the moon's surface, planting an American flag and signaling victory in the space race.

Why Benefits Matter

Let's bring this back down from the moon.

Starting in grade school, we learn that we experience the world through our five senses. What we see, hear, feel, smell, and taste make up how we get around this planet. The sky is blue, thunder is loud, summer is warm, flowers smell good, and candy tastes sweet. It's a pretty good life out there.

So naturally when we want to tell people about something, our default path is to tune in to those senses and describe the facts. We use our sight to look at the new television we bought and marvel at the crisp colors. We'll rave about the heated seats in our car or compliment the minty aroma of a fresh tube of toothpaste.

These details describe material truths. They paint a picture of the world as it is. But when we're tasked with moving people to action, we can't rely on these senses alone—they're only half of the equation. If we truly want to move people, we must get deeper into what actually motivates us. And as it turns out, there is a secret blueprint for developing simple, effective messages that do just that.

In the first part of this book, we learned *why* simplicity is effective, and in this part, we'll dive into *how*, equipping ourselves with a tool kit that gets us there. To start, we'll examine our motivations.

The Drill

Let's say you work for a big tool company. Every day, you walk in, stroll past the assembly lines on the factory floor, and hike the stairs up to your office. Then, settling into your desk, you see today's first assignment: craft an ad for the company's newest line of cordless drills.

Balanced by its hefty battery pack, this bright orange and black tool sits on your desk, and you pick it up to take a closer look. The engineers worked hard to squeeze more torque out of this one, and when you pull the trigger you can feel the powerful motor spin. Down the hall, the design team tested hundreds of handles to find the most ergonomic grip. You scribble down a couple of notes, and after noodling on it for a few minutes, you type: "Now with 20 percent more power, a new ultra-comfort silicone grip, and improved 8-hour battery life, the SimpleDrill 3000 is the best tool for homeowners and construction pros alike." Seems good enough, let's send the ad off to print.

All these facts are true. The product is better than ever. But that ad sucks.

That's an ad that doesn't understand why people buy drills. That's a message that comes from just opening up the window of those five senses, taking in a few facts, adding a splash of color, and seeing what comes out.

We don't buy drills because they have more torque, comfortable handles, or a longer battery life.

Why do we buy drills? Legendary marketing professor Theodore Levitt best summarizes the reason: "People don't want to buy a quarter-inch drill. They want a quarter-inch hole!"[4]

Last year, customers worldwide bought $10 billion worth of power drills. But not a single one of those customers actually wanted a drill. They wanted a hole.

What we experience with our five senses—the drill's size and shape, its performance, and its functions—are important to us only because they help us get what we actually want. We don't want the thing, we want what the thing does for us. Understanding this is the first step in our blueprint.

What Do We Actually Want?

The drill and the hole illustrate a fundamental truth about how we make decisions. Every single time somebody has ever tried to get you to do anything, be it buy a product, vote for a candidate, donate to a cause, or even just take out the overflowing garbage bag, a voice in your head is asking one question: "What's in it for me?" Sometimes the "me" is ourselves, while other times the "me" is our community. Sometimes that voice is screaming, and other times it speaks at just a whisper.

Ultimately, we only ever do things because we somehow want the *result* of that thing.

In all our choices, we seek benefits, not features. Features exist in the five senses. Benefits are how those features bring value to our lives. When we frame our messaging around benefits, we tell people why they should give a damn.

The best salespeople in the world know this. The best leaders in the world know this. And it works for arenas far beyond the hardware store.

The good news is we can easily uncover the benefits of anything we're trying to pitch by asking a simple question: "So what?" The drill has a longer battery life. So what? The car has heated seats. So what? The toothpaste has a minty flavor. So what?

The drill's longer battery life means you can drill more holes without stopping. The car's heated seats mean you can keep your butt nice and toasty. The toothpaste's minty flavor means you'll have fresher breath.

These features already feel more vivid and enticing than when we just listed them before. But here's what the most effective communicators do: they ask that question again. "So what?"

The drill's longer battery life means you can drill more holes without stopping, which means you can get those family photos on the wall sooner. The car's heated seats mean you can keep your butt nice and toasty, which means you can have a relaxing, comfortable ride. The toothpaste's minty flavor means you'll have fresher breath, which means you'll make a good impression on that first date.

With these changes, we see what's in it for us. These features aren't just bullet points on a brochure, they are keys to us having a better life. Digging deeper helps us connect deeper.

We call these two layers the *functional benefits* and *emotional benefits*. At the first level, functional benefits describe what changes in the objective world as a result of your offering—what is the advantage it gives the receiver? At the second level, emotional benefits describe what changes in the receiver's subjective world—how are they better off because of this feature? How does it make them feel?

Let's look at an example of how this plays out in another domain, the thorny arena of public health. A number of studies have repeatedly shown that our consumption of high-calorie snacks, what we dub "junk food," is not only bad for our individual health but can also be quite a drag on our collective medical infrastructure. Some estimates of the cost of our junk food obsession peg the tally as high as $50 billion a year (though my personal guilty favorite, Auntie Anne's pretzels, might just be worth the bill).

With stakes this high, anything we can do to get us to cut back on this snacking can have a big impact, and governments around the world have begun trying hard to nudge us in that direction. In Philadelphia, policymakers instituted a tax on high-sugar soft drinks, which has caused their consumption to dip by an average of 22 percent. In Mexico, a similar tax reduced sales by as much as 12 percent. Considering that the average American adult consumes seventy-seven grams of sugar per day (up to three times the recommended total), these numbers are significant.[5]

In a 2022 study, researchers from Oxford and Cambridge surveyed thousands of respondents in the United Kingdom about a hypothetical policy designed to reduce the consumption of junk food, aiming to see how different types of messages would influence public support.[6] They found that support for the idea varied significantly based on how much the message focused on benefits.

In their first group, the control, they just stated the facts of the fictional policy to figure out a baseline level of support. Their prompt was "Imagine the government is considering a new policy to increase the price of high calorie snacks by 10 percent to help people eat less."

Solely on its own merits, 37 percent of those surveyed supported the policy as is.

Then the researchers framed the initiative in a slightly different way, asking another group about the same policy, but this time including the desired outcome, which we can map to the functional benefit in our model: "Imagine the government is considering a new policy to increase the price of high calorie snacks by 10 percent to help people eat less. Research shows that the introduction of this new policy will reduce the number of high calorie snacks people eat."

Despite this inclusion of a first-level, functional benefit, support stayed pretty much the same, at 36 percent.

Then, with one small tweak, everything changed. In the next group, they finally hit pay dirt by outlining the benefits of this policy, rotating their description between three different next-level benefits: "Imagine the government is considering a new policy to increase the price of high calorie snacks by 10 percent to help people eat less. Research shows that the introduction of this new policy will reduce the number of high calorie snacks people eat. This will cut [the number of people who get cancer *or* National *or* National Health Service costs *or* environmental harms]."

As soon as an emotional benefit entered into the equation, support for this policy increased by a full one-third, to 48 percent of respondents. And when they tested a message that combined all three benefits, support for the imaginary junk food tax hit 54 percent, a firm majority. Incredibly, changing just a few words can turn a long-shot proposal into a winning idea—in this case, one that can ultimately save lives. When the same researchers studied similar messaging patterns for alcohol or meat consumption and policies that restricted availability instead of raising taxes, they saw the same pattern emerge time and again. Stating the benefits, not just the features, increases buy-in.

What Do We Actually Need?

Peeling back those first couple of layers is a good start, but we haven't hit the bedrock yet. We have to unearth the ultimate desires that are making us tick. Only then will we uncover the last pieces of our blueprint.

In a world with more than 350 million products on Amazon, we might think that there is an infinite number of different wants and needs. Despite this incredible selection brought to us by the miracles of a boundless internet, everything that you or I have ever wanted can be categorized into just five major buckets.

Studying human behavior in the early half of the twentieth century, psychologist Abraham Maslow became curious about what motivates people to do what they do. This idea was novel, as up till then the prevailing focus of psychology was all about illness. Maslow would later say about the father of psychoanalysis Sigmund Freud, "It is as if Freud supplied us the sick half of psychology and we must now fill it out with the healthy half." In 1943, as he pursued this new humanistic study of motivation, Maslow introduced one of the most influential ideas in all social sciences: his hierarchy of needs.[7]

You've likely seen this model before. It's often represented as a colorful pyramid or staircase, as shown in figure 4.1, and can be found in a thousand textbooks or management presentations, and for a good reason: it still works. Maslow's insights on our basic needs have largely stood the test of time (of course, with a few tweaks or critiques here and there) and with their help, we can uncover why some messages do the same.

According to this model, we all have a set of universal needs that we try to fulfill in our lives. Everything we ever want can be categorized as physiological, safety, love and belonging, esteem, and self-actualization needs:

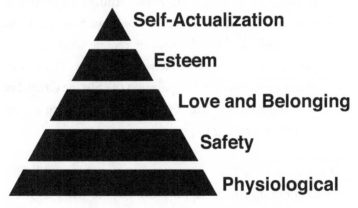

Figure 4.1. Maslow's hierarchy of needs.

+ *Physiological*—Before anything else, we have to take care of our biological necessities. We need food when we're hungry, water when we're thirsty, shelter and clothing when we're cold, sleep when we're tired, and sex, well, when we're horny.
+ *Safety*—We seek self-preservation and safety in all its forms. This bucket covers our health, physical security, emotional security, and financial security.
+ *Love and belonging*—These needs make us human. We crave the love of our family and friends and the belonging of being part of a group. We are all looking for intimacy, trust, acceptance, and affection.
+ *Esteem*—Our esteem need comes in two subcategories: how we view ourselves and how others view us. In the first, we're looking inward for strength, competence, mastery, and achievement. Then, from society, we seek respect, reputation, status, and prestige.
+ *Self-actualization*—The highest level of our needs is a broad category that includes everything related to realizing our full potential. At our best, we aim to achieve great goals, build and create incredible work, grow as people, and express ourselves creatively. These successes can be as grand as painting the Sistine Chapel or winning a Nobel Prize or as everyday as being a great parent or learning to play the guitar.

Generally, we all try to meet each need in roughly this order to climb up the metaphorical ladder to the next need, but this progression is not as clear-cut as a video game, and we tend to skip around a bit. In fact, despite being most popularly represented as a pyramid, Maslow never illustrated his hierarchy in that manner. For our purposes, however, we're just interested in the foundational categories themselves.

The most effective messages all boil down to one of these fundamental needs, which can help us identify the final layer of "So what?" Let's look at how they relate to some of the examples we've seen before.

The drill's longer battery life means you can drill more holes without stopping, which means you can get those family photos on the wall sooner, which helps you meet your love and belonging needs.

The car's heated seats mean that you can keep your butt nice and toasty, which means you can have a relaxing and comfortable ride, which helps you meet your physiological needs.

The toothpaste's minty flavor means you'll have fresher breath, which means you'll make a good impression on that first date, which helps you meet your esteem needs.

We did it. We hit bedrock. After three levels of interrogation, we fully understand why these features actually matter. And with this established understanding as our base, we can begin to build our message back up. The most effective communicators use this simple model to persuade and tell their stories. We'll call it the Drill-Build method.

Getting Beneficial

The journey we've taken so far—from the features we can see and feel, through the first-level functional benefits, past the second-level emotional benefits, and finally down to the foundational need—helps us establish a blueprint for structuring

Examples of Beneficial and Nonbeneficial Messages

"1,000 songs in your pocket."
  —Apple

"Music the way it wants to be."
  —Microsoft

"Be all that you can be."
  —US Army

"Army of One."
  —US Army

"Early to bed, early to rise, makes a man healthy, wealthy, and wise."
  —Benjamin Franklin

"Sleep plays a vital role in good health and well-being throughout your life."
  —National Heart, Lung, and Blood Institute

a clear, compelling message. The best part is, you don't have to be a master builder to follow these plans. Let's do it together.

Drill, Then Build

Like a skyscraper must dig down into the earth to secure its structure, we look at the need to help us anchor our message to establish the *direction*. And like the basement in a building, we don't see this layer above the surface. We can do this using the Drill-Build method, shown in figure 4.2.

Let's go back to our example of the cordless drill. We've established that the need we're addressing is love and belonging. We don't go plastering this on our packaging or website, but it helps us choose our direction and tone, which we'll say is sentimental.

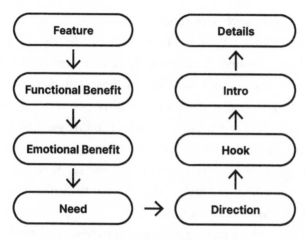

Figure 4.2. Drill-Build method.

With this information, we start crafting our message. We begin by working our way back up, matching each level across to the corresponding item. Our *hook*, which is that first line on our website, introduction in our speech, or headline on our ad, is based on an emotional benefit. For our drill, the emotional benefit is that it allows us to put family photos on the wall. For our hook, we can say something such as "Save your memories."

The hook helps get the attention of your audience, and once you do, we move on to what you say next, your intro. Here, you need to lock in your audience by referring back to your functional benefit.

We identified the functional benefit of our drill's longer battery life as getting more done without stopping, so we can reframe that into an intro along the lines of "Get that whole gallery wall up in just one afternoon with the SimpleDrill 3000's all-day battery life."

With this, we have captured the reader's attention, have explained what's in it for them, and can finally get to the *details*, the features themselves. By catching the eye of those who matter to us and weeding out those who don't, we now have the luxury of getting into the nitty-gritty, talking about the drill's 20 percent larger battery, comfort grip, and extra power. Using the Drill-Build method, we've reshaped our messsage to make it more persuasive, and set ourselves up to sell a whole lot more tools. Take a look at the before and after versions shown in figure 4.3.

One of these messages jumbles up a bunch of details and blends in with the rest of the noise in our busy lives. The other one tells a story about why people actually want this product. Now that you know this model, you'll see it everywhere great communicators do their work.

But unfortunately, oftentimes we see some of the biggest players forget this simple framework. When they do, you'll see eager competitors who do get it right on their tail, giving them a run for their money.

Keep Your Eye on the Prize

The older you get, the bigger you get, and the more you are removed from the hole and focus on the drill. Established players in business and other arenas can easily forget what got them where they are and begin to take their message for granted, possibly thinking, "Hey, if everybody knows who we are, why should we bother investing in telling a good story?"

Developing a beneficial message is often easier when you are a hotshot challenger—you're simply closer to the motivation

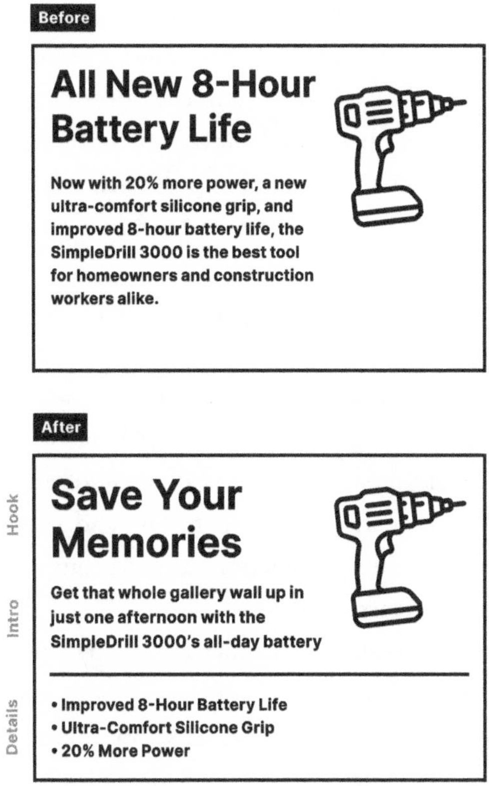

Before

All New 8-Hour Battery Life

Now with 20% more power, a new ultra-comfort silicone grip, and improved 8-hour battery life, the SimpleDrill 3000 is the best tool for homeowners and construction workers alike.

After

Hook

Save Your Memories

Intro

Get that whole gallery wall up in just one afternoon with the SimpleDrill 3000's all-day battery

Details

• Improved 8-Hour Battery Life
• Ultra-Comfort Silicone Grip
• 20% More Power

Figure 4.3. Before and after organizing our message using the Drill-Build method.

that drives the story. Let's look at some brands that have lost the plot and those that are telling a better narrative while nipping at their heels.

Before 2010, the eyeglasses industry was stagnant and monopolistic, with one major player controlling everything from production to branding to distribution. Bursting onto the scene, Warby Parker turned this world on its head by introducing a range of stylish, low-cost frames and a convenient online shopping experience. Since then, it's made a sizable chink in the establishment's armor, grown to a multibillion dollar valuation, and even taken the leap from pixels and code to brick and mortar by opening over 150 physical stores—inspiring dozens of like-minded direct-to-consumer challengers across similarly staid industries in the process.

Warby Parker's biggest competitor is LensCrafters, owned by the gargantuan eyewear conglomerate Luxottica. Note how LensCrafters communicates with this line pulled from its home page: "Take care of your eyes with our wide range of vision solutions. Choose from an assortment of quality lenses and the latest eyewear collections online and in-store now." Quality lenses and fresh collections are nice, but is that really why you buy the glasses you buy?

Compare that to how its challenger Warby Parker does it: "Buying eyewear should leave you happy and good-looking, with money in your pocket. Glasses, sunglasses, and contacts—we've got your eyes covered." Makes you feel something, right? We see the emotional benefits up front. We're buying glasses from Warby because they make us "happy and good-looking."

Let's shift to something many of us spend a lot of time looking at through those glasses: spreadsheets. Since its introduction in 1987, Microsoft Excel is perhaps the most successful software product of all time, serving as both a backbone of the modern enterprise and a valuable tool for church groups, soccer leagues, academic researchers, and a thousand other uses. Unfortunately, it's become so entrenched in our infrastructure that it appears Microsoft has forgotten how to talk about it.

On its website, here are some of the first words that Microsoft says about one of its most important products. First, a distribution feature: "Get it now with a Microsoft 365 subscription." Then, a product feature: "Enhanced by intelligence for experts and novices." These messages don't tell you what the product is for or why you should care.

A new cohort of tools is quickly coming up on the side of Excel; the most notable among them is Airtable, founded in 2012. In addition to including new features that better fit how many of this generation's businesses are using spreadsheets, Airtable's superpower is in its simple messaging. Here's what it leads with: "Connect everything. Achieve anything. Accelerate work and unlock potential with powerful apps that connect your data, workflows and teams." Don't you immediately understand how its product can help you?

Funny enough, Microsoft wasn't always this dull. If we look back to the first ad for Excel, we see it start, "Introducing Microsoft Excel. The soul of the new machines." It goes on to list the benefits later in the copy: "Microsoft Excel can help you in ways that no spreadsheet ever could before. With instantly impressive output. Speed that never lets you miss a beat. And features that let Microsoft Excel adapt to your needs instead of the other way around."

Time and scale can create distance between senders and receivers. That distance makes the benefits seem blurrier and blurrier with each step—while the features stay in focus. By deliberately pushing ourselves to interrogate why our message matters, we're able to better connect.

Some of what we've uncovered here may seem obvious. You didn't buy this book because you wanted a couple hundred pieces of paper in some binding. When you ordered your coffee this morning, you knew that you wanted the caffeine kick, not just some hot water poured over roasted beans. You may look at the "Before" ad for the drill in figure 4.3 and say, "Nah, nobody would say things like this. Of course the pros would say it better." But the obvious can be easy to miss, and simple is harder than it looks—especially without the right framework. To see how much untapped opportunity there is for structured messaging, all you have to do is look at the actual language attached to some of the most popular cordless drills among those millions of products on Amazon:

> The BLACK+DECKER 20V MAX cordless drill/driver is up to the challenge of quick home repairs, DIY projects, and more. Use this compact, cordless drill/driver on wood, metal, and plastic. It's designed with a 24-position clutch that helps keep you from stripping and overdriving screws for enhanced control over every project. The soft-grip handle provides the comfort you need from start to finish, while the rechargeable 20V MAX POWERCONNECT battery can even be used with other tools within the POWERCONNECT system.[8]

We can do better than that. Research proves it, history proves it, and now you know how to do it. We don't want a drill. We don't want a hole. We don't want the photos on the wall. We want love and belonging. The drill just helps us get there.

The Work

- Audit your existing messaging. Are you leading with benefits or features?
- How is the receiver's life better for hearing your message? What pain did you solve?
- What do you want them to do with your message? What's the action step?
- Ask yourself, "So what?" "So what?" "So what?" What do you uncover at each level? Which level makes sense for you to invest in?
- Stress test your message. What's the biggest objection your receiver could have? How do you respond to it?

5

Focused:
Fighting the
Frankenstein Idea

Thou shalt not follow a multitude to do evil.

—Exodus

E very semester I have my marketing students form agencies
to work on several group projects. In the first assignment,
they have to work together to develop a pitch for a brand that
I brief them on, and I bring in some other marketing professionals to help play the role of client, give feedback, and pick
a winning proposal.

Now, many of my students do brilliant work. But every
single time, I see in these undergrads the same fatal error that
even seasoned executives fall victim to: the Frankenstein idea.

In Mary Shelley's pioneering horror novel, Dr. Victor Frankenstein develops a process for breathing life into nonliving beings and sets forth on creating a living man, "the Creature."[1] This is how the result is described:

> His limbs were in proportion, and I had selected his features as beautiful. Beautiful! Great God! His yellow skin scarcely covered the work of muscles and arteries beneath; his hair was of a lustrous black, and flowing; his teeth of a pearly whiteness; but these luxuriances only formed a more horrid contrast with his watery eyes, that seemed almost of the same colour as the dun-white sockets in which they were set, his shrivelled complexion and straight black lips.

Dr. Frankenstein deliberately picked beautiful individual pieces of anatomy, but when he assembled this collection of mismatched components, what awoke was a hideous monster. Each part formed a "horrid contrast" with the others, and the whole was far worse than the sum of its parts.

This same mad science happens whenever groups of people are brought together to form ideas. Somebody throws out the thought of using influencers, another person shouts "drones," NFTs and AI enter the conversation, and three different hashtags appear on the whiteboard. The deadline comes, everything is mashed together, and the final project is a seven-headed monster.

These never work.

You cannot be everything to everybody. You cannot say two things at once. Whenever you try, you will fail.

Why Focus Matters

Frankenstein ideas are fundamentally unfocused.

When you have one big point, people can't help but notice it. But when you have four or five crammed in there, they can easily lose the plot. Every time you add something else, you decrease the emphasis on what's there already. The zero-sum pie of our attention gets sliced thinner and thinner, illustrated in figure 5.1.

This isn't just a problem of losing a little bit of effectiveness though. Losing focus is a problem of what engineers call *catastrophic failure*, when everything breaks at once.

If you try to juggle too many balls, you don't just drop the last one. They all fall. When your message doesn't pierce the shield of indifference or reach a critical mass, it doesn't work just a bit less—it fails completely. Our brains just aren't wired to give attention to multiple inputs simultaneously. For almost all of us, 97.5 percent to be exact, multitasking is a myth.[2] Unless we're one of the rare "supertaskers" who buck this trend, rapidly switching our attention from one task or idea to another hurts our ability to give any its proper weight.

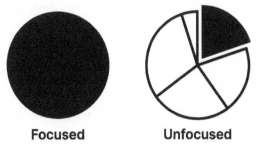

Focused   **Unfocused**

Figure 5.1. Attention is zero-sum.

When you force that divided attention by failing to focus your message, you then fail to connect altogether. An old bit of folk wisdom sums this up perfectly: "When you chase two rabbits, you catch none."

The word *priority* is singular. You can attend to only one idea first—and ultimately, you can do only one thing best. The *and-and-and*s that we so readily pursue, both in our solo work and with others, all push us in the other direction. Focus is an uphill battle.

Committees Kill Greatness

If Frankenstein's monster is the most cursed creation in literature, committees are the most gruesome foe in the business world. The very word conjures up visions of fluorescent conference rooms and stale bagels, endless Zoom calls and glitchy screen-shares. They are hard to love.

Writer G. K. Chesterton reportedly said, "I've searched all the parks in all the cities—and found no statues of committees." British civil servant Barnett Cocks is said to have used this definition: "A committee is a cul-de-sac down which ideas are lured and then quietly strangled."

Research shows that group brainstorms, designed to spark creativity and generate ideas, often do just the opposite. In both quality and quantity of output, individuals frequently outperform groups—and meetings tend to get worse the bigger they are. According to studies of these dynamics, once you get past about six or seven people in a group, you hit a ceiling on total ideas being shared over the course of a meeting.[3] Introverts have a hard time getting heard, and a single loudmouth can derail the entire conversation.

Don't get me wrong—collaboration can and often is essential and wonderful and has been the seed of many incredible achievements in art, business, science, and everywhere else humans put their efforts. This tool belongs in our kit, and indeed, we'll talk a great deal about how vital working with others is later on in this book. But we're also going to point to the perils of getting it wrong, which we're apt to do.

Committees, when they lack purpose and leadership, are machines of mediocrity, creators of complication. Far more often will a brilliant, simple message be killed by group dynamics than will that group produce something great of its own. Iconic adman David Ogilvy said, "Committees can criticize ... but they should never be allowed to create."[4]

Simple messages, by virtue of being high-contrast and standing out from the crowd, take bravery. Bravery is already a tall order by yourself but is particularly hard to come by in a group, where all incentives point toward making the safe bet. Groups revert to the mean, optimizing for minimal risk and shaving off all the interesting bits—the bits that make your message work.

Less Is Painful

"Stuff" has advocates. The lack of stuff generally doesn't. In the boardroom or in the newspaper, we all love to proudly point to a feature we added, a bridge we built, or an idea we brought to life. But in the best-case scenario, the absence of something doesn't have a champion (see figure 5.2)—and harder yet, defenders of the stuff often stand in the way, protecting their legacy and their salary. Legal departments want you to hedge your claims, internal teams want their features shown in the commercial, and CEOs want to see their face

Figure 5.2. There is no evidence of absence.

on the website. Everybody wants something in, and nobody wants something taken out.

Cutting and distilling your message is inherently painful. It means you need to make trade-offs, that some things get included and others do not. The pain is both internal and external. We hate to "kill our darlings." And our collaborators much prefer when their *stuff* is in the former category—and they will fight to keep it there. It's self-preservation.

You have to push through this pain to take flight. To achieve focus you need creative authority, you need vision, you need to understand how to play the politics of less, and most of all, you need to commit.

Getting Focused

Focus requires us to make choices, manage trade-offs, and sell our ideas. Often this involves less about knowing the nuances of language, imagery, or structure and more about understanding people and their incentives. To reach our

Examples of Focused and Unfocused Messages

"Save money. Live better."
  —Walmart

"There's more for your life at Sears."
  —Sears

"Have it your way."
  —Burger King

"Eatin' good in the neighborhood."
  —Applebee's

"Absence makes the heart grow fonder."
  —Folk Wisdom

"Absence, communication, kindness, and affection make the heart grow fonder."
  —Not Folk Wisdom

receiver, we need to do the internal work of becoming a focused sender.

Replace *And* with *So*

First in our fight for simplicity, we have to plant a flag: the word *and* is the enemy. *And* shoots too wide; *and* means something else. Instead, in your planning and thinking, replace it with *so*. *So* means that one idea flows from another and that a direct causal relationship and lineage exists between your big idea and how you bring it to life.

The goal "We are going to develop a loyalty program for our café and release a line of collectible coffee mugs" sounds like a complete, grammatically correct English sentence. No alarm bells go off. Our brains hear it and think, "Oh yeah, that makes sense" and move on. But let's swap the *and* for *so* and try it again: "We are going to develop a loyalty program for our café, so we'll release a line of collectible coffee mugs."

That sounds a little clunkier, right? What do the mugs have to do with the loyalty program exactly? A flag goes up in our heads, and we realize that these two things aren't really related—this is a Frankenstein idea in the making. Going back to the drawing board, we're better off with this idea: "We are going to develop a loyalty program for our café, so we will build a mobile app to allow customers to track points."

That makes a lot more sense. That's one solid idea, not three ideas in a trenchcoat.

Compare "We are doing *idea x* and *tactic y*" with "We are doing *idea x*, so *tactic y*," also shown in figure 5.3.

And is like the tape and string that my grandfather used to use to fix things and put pieces together that don't quite fit right. You can attach a lot of ideas that shouldn't go together with an *and*, making them look like they "kinda sorta work" by doing so. Frankenstein's monster is sewn together by *ands*.

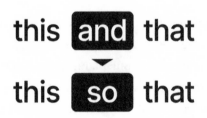

Figure 5.3. Test the cohesiveness of your message by replacing *and* with *so*.

But *so* makes you think. *So* means that you need to develop a clear path from the first idea you say to the second one. If your story doesn't make sense with a *so*, it just doesn't make sense.

Have a Boss

Rock 'n' roll is a tough business. To succeed in the long run, it takes both creative brilliance and the business chops to keep everything together.

Over five decades, Bruce Springsteen has arguably been the most successful rock star in history. The Grammy, Oscar, Tony, Golden Globe, and Presidential Medal of Freedom recipient from New Jersey is enshrined in both the Songwriters Hall of Fame and Rock and Roll Hall of Fame. Now in his seventies, he continues to sell out stadiums and top the charts with each new album. There are many icons out there, but without question Bruuuuce (as he's often referred to by a screaming crowd) is firmly on rock's Mount Rushmore.

In his 2016 memoir *Born to Run*, Springsteen discusses the windy road that led him to the peak of his craft. His first band, the Castiles, was energetic but chaotic. They'd butt heads over pretty much everything, and members of the group repeatedly spent time in and out of police custody. Though they had some success in the local clubs and even cut a single, things were just too messy to last. Ultimately, the band had too many rockers and not enough leaders.

Years later, after some time playing solo, Springsteen began to assemble what he now calls the "heart-stopping, pants-dropping, house-rocking, earth-quaking, booty-shaking,

Viagra-taking, love-making, legendary E Street Band!" But unlike the Castiles, Springsteen isn't *in* the E Street Band—instead, it's *his* band. Here's how he describes the process: "In the beginning I knew I wanted something more than a solo act and less than a one-man-one-vote democratic band. I'd been there and it didn't fit me. Democracy in rock bands, with very few exceptions, is often a ticking time bomb."[5]

Bruce Springsteen's nickname is "The Boss," and for a good reason. He's in charge. It's his creative vision, it's his decision who is in and who is out, and it's his job to make sure everything hums (and everything rocks). His name is in lights, but it's also his responsibility.

Too many organizations lack this authority. These inherently flat student groups in my class are ripe for this trap—but so are a lot of collaborations far beyond the classroom. Any group without a leader or an agreed-on process for making decisions and a single person bearing the ownership of success or failure can easily fall into chaos when the first bit of friction appears. That chaos is the enemy of focus.

The best way out of this mess involves instituting creative leadership. Sometimes consensus is possible, but most of the time, somebody must ultimately have the authority to stare at that messy list of ideas, toss the ones that don't work, and draw a big fat circle around the winner.

This work is hard. Being the decider is a thankless job. You just taped a giant target on your back for when things inevitably get rough down the road, and you probably pissed off everybody except the contributors that developed the winning concept. Taking on this role, even with its pains, is worthwhile and necessary to develop winning, focused ideas.

Creative work and effective ideas are almost always the result of influences and collaborations with our communities, teams, and the world around us. There is no such thing as the lone genius creating in a vacuum—that image is total fiction. But what is true in all effective collaborations is the decidedly unsexy act of editing. Everything can't be a winner, and somebody has to be trusted to make that call.

Having a leader doesn't mean having a dictator; it means having a facilitator. A good boss, empowered to make decisions, helps organize us and brings out the best we have to offer.

Be Explicit in Your Instructions

In chapter 3, we learned that our default is to want and do more. When we're faced with an open-ended problem, our first instinct is to add elements to reach our goal—Lego and colored squares in the lab experiments, and words, slides, and web pages in our professional world.

The researchers behind that study shared in Leidy Klotz's book *Subtract* discovered one foolproof remedy to this: simply tell people that subtraction is allowed.[6] In the studies where participants modified Lego structures, when experimenters added a single line of instruction that reminded people they could remove blocks to get to their goal, the number that did just that increased by twenty percentage points. When they ran the same type of experiment for subjects designing an imaginary minigolf course, the share that used subtraction jumped by twenty-seven points. A gentle nudge of "Hey, less is an option too" is enough to completely change how we think and act.

Explicitly reminding people that simplifying is an option increases their mental availability of that idea. *Availability bias* describes how easily we can reach for an idea, memory, or concept. If you just went for a hike this weekend, you're predisposed to suggest hiking when you are asked to recommend a form of exercise. If you're a defense attorney, you're more apt to tell a pollster that crime is a big problem in your city. In these examples, hiking and crime are within easy grasp in our brains—they are more accessible. The more that simplicity is at the front of our minds, the more likely we are to pick up that tool and use it on the problem at hand.

Tell people that simplifying is an option and show them how focus matters, and you've primed them for choosing this path. Everything else gets a lot easier once this option is conspicuously unlocked.

Understand the Politics

Let's go back to the Boss for a moment. Springsteen has a line of simple wisdom that he likes to share at his concerts: "Nobody wins unless everybody wins."

The Boss was talking more about building a just and fair society than corporate decision-making, but the message still applies. The fundamental guiding value in getting buy-in for your ideas and for the often-painful process of simplifying is helping everybody win. It's politics 101.

Every stakeholder that you need to convince has differing motivations. Some make a lot of sense, such as the CEO wanting to look good for the board—and the board wanting the stock price to go up. Some are less directly tied to a nominal mission, such as a developer wanting to have an easier task updating the app or a manager wanting some big headline metrics to help their case for a promotion. And further still, some motivations are completely separate from what's stated on the tin. Sometimes your CMO hates the guts of some rival executive or a copywriter has a lucky word they like to include in their work. Your job as a change agent is to understand this landscape and help find a way for everybody to see your work as a win for them.

This may seem a little icky to some people. You may not like to "play politics," and you're not alone in that. In a survey by recruiting firm Robert Half, 43 percent of workers prefer to "stay completely out of the fray" when it comes to politics.[7] But they are present whether you like it or not, and you are affected by them whether you play along or not. Any time people gather to work together, there are motivations and there are politics. Politics is just the process of navigating those waters.

As vice chairman of Ogilvy, Rory Sutherland has spent his career selling innovative (and sometimes crazy) ideas to some of the biggest clients in the world. In his book *Alchemy*, about the magic of these often illogical and counterintuitive concepts, he explains the secret behind getting sign-off on big ideas: "Remember what often matters most to those making a decision in business or government is not a successful outcome, but their ability to defend their decisions, whatever the outcome may be."[8]

Most people in a large organization just want cover. They want to be able to justify their decisions to their bosses, voters, or shareholders and to live to see another day. They want that target off their backs. When you are pitching a new and scary idea—the idea of focused "less"—you need to give them the permission to take that risk.

Point to the research and examples in this book or others on your shelf. Find statistics that back you up or experts you can cite. Polish up your own credentials and get buy-in from stakeholders up and down the chain. Simplicity means having fewer places to hide, but to get there, you'll need to make everybody feel safe in the process. Do your homework, work the room, and bring people with you.

Commit

After you've done all of that—when you've empowered a leader, set the table, and played the politics—you are still going to face one last hurdle in your fight to focus your messaging: making a final choice. You'll sit there, with option A and option B staring at you from a computer screen, and you'll need to make a call.

You don't want to make the wrong choice. Maybe you're about to update the front page of your website, the first crucial impression of your brand to thousands of visitors a day. Or maybe you're about to drop a check to spend millions to launch a presidential campaign. The stakes are high, and the decision is paralyzing. Which is the right slogan? Which call to action will work?

That's hard to say with certainty, but there is one universal bad choice: not choosing.

Inaction and indecisiveness are how we get a muddled, complicated world where everything is for everybody but nothing means anything. Done is king. Make a choice, and embrace it. Voltaire said, "Perfect is the enemy of the good."[9] In marketing, entrepreneurship, and everywhere else we communicate, there is no perfect. Taking the "good" and running with it is far better than sitting at the starting line, afraid to hit the gas.

The very act of committing is part of the secret. A whole-hearted effort behind a simple but mediocre idea defeats a clumsy attempt to bring a Frankenstein idea to life. In the real world outside of Mary Shelley's imagination, it doesn't matter how many volts you pulse through that hideous creature—it's not waking up.

Like the adage about those two rabbits that we can fruit-lessly chase, football coaches have an old saying, "When you have two quarterbacks, you have none." You can't go into a game without committing to a choice. You can't have success without decisiveness and clarity.

But what if people hate it? Good. The distance between love and hate is a lot shorter than the gulf between apathy and passion. If they hate your stuff, if your message rubs them the wrong way, at least they care about you and your idea. Breaking through from indifference to attention is more than half the battle.

Red Bull routinely scored miserably on taste tests but has built a devoted following as one of the top beverage brands in the world. The Eiffel Tower was called a "half-built factory pipe, a carcass waiting to be fleshed out with freestone or brick, a funnel-shaped grill, a hole-riddled suppository" and is now the most visited monument on the planet.[10] When you commit, people tend to come around.

Communicating with one core idea that you've gone deep on is always better than five half-assed concepts that you taped together. And here's the dirty secret about that one idea: it doesn't even have to be that good! A mediocre concept that has been competently executed beats a muddled mix of otherwise brilliant ideas with no follow-through or unifying connection. Focus itself makes your work better.

The Work

- How many rabbits are you chasing? Count the *ands* in your message. How many can be removed?
- Who stands to benefit from your message being effective? Who stands to benefit from the status quo? How can you move those in the latter group to the former?
- If your receiver feels only one emotion, what would it be?
- How accessible is more? How accessible is less? What can you do to make them more balanced?

6

Salient:
Constraints
Breed Creativity

*I have made this longer than usual because
I have not had time to make it shorter.*

—Blaise Pascal

"Dick said, 'Look, look. Look up. Look up, up, up.' Jane said, 'Run, run. Run, Dick, run. Run and see.'"

For millions of students in the middle of the twentieth century, the tales of siblings Dick and Jane were the definitive early reader book. At one point, 85 percent of American elementary schools used them in their curriculum.[1]

But everybody hated them. In *Life* magazine, they were critiqued as "insipid illustrations depicting the slicked-up lives of other children. . . . All feature abnormally courteous, unnaturally clean boys and girls." Students, parents, and educators alike would describe the books as terminally boring, vapid, and even biased—and the white-bread books would fail in their stated goal, getting children interested in reading.

On the contrary, if there is somebody whose work could never be called boring, it was Theodor Geisel, better known to children and former children around the globe as Dr. Seuss. Through more than half a billion copies of his sixty-plus books, he has likely shaped more young minds than just about anybody in history. He was the first author I ever read, and the odds are pretty good it might be the same for you.

Fed up with Dick and Jane, as well as other dull early reader primers of the day, Seuss's publisher challenged him to write "a story that first-graders can't put down!" The prolific author accepted, and to push it a step further, he gave himself a constraint—limit the vocabulary to just a list of a couple hundred words important to those young readers.[2]

It wasn't easy. Seuss sweated it out for a year and a half. Eventually, he developed an iconic story of chaos, authority, and mischief that clocked in at a measly 236 different words.[3] A complete departure from the polished suburban dreamscape home of Dick and Jane, the instantly loved *The Cat in the Hat* was born.

Shortly after that release, Seuss doubled down. His publisher bet him fifty dollars that he could not write a book using just fifty words from that same list. It was a bad bet. After toiling away for another year, in 1960 Seuss published the equally zany *Green Eggs and Ham*, his most successful title ever, weighing in right at that total word count.

By imposing constraints on his work, Seuss was able to create unique work that became the two most successful titles of his long career, and in turn inspired generations of young minds. He was able to create something different and impossible to ignore by playing a different game than everybody else.

Near the end of his life, Seuss looked back and gloated about this success: "I think one of the happiest things I've done is getting rid of Dick and Jane."[4] By embracing the power of creative pressure in our own work, we can also get away from the same old, same old, and communicate in a way that's impossible to ignore.

Why Salience Matters

Simple messages are salient, which means they stand out. Salient things stick out, stand above, jump up, or otherwise contrast with their surroundings—and thus rise to our attention.

Our perception of the world around us is largely determined by what's salient. And what's salient is determined not by the message or object itself but by how it differs from its environment. We need to differentiate the figure from the background to see, hear, and understand the world around us.

If you're sitting in a classroom and suddenly a disco ball turns on, you'll immediately notice it. But if you're in a nightclub, you probably wouldn't bat an eye when one starts to spin. Conversely, if you saw somebody at that club reading a book, you'd notice that a lot quicker than if you saw them doing the same thing on campus. A parka looks suspicious on the beach, and a bathing suit looks bananas on the ski slope. Using slang in a business proposal is novel and attention-grabbing in the same way that using a PowerPoint deck on a dating profile is.

We notice, and often choose, what's different, like in figure 6.1. An entire genre of books hit the bestseller lists in the past decade with titles that stand out on a shelf full of blasé motivational and business jargon: *The Subtle Art of Not Giving a F*ck* by Mark Manson, *You Are a Badass* by Jen Sincero, and *Unfu*k Yourself* by Gary John Bishop among many others. Using expletives makes these titles novel and noticeable, in turn making the ears of readers perk up and winning that first wedge of attention. When cryptocurrency platform Coinbase aired a startlingly simple Super Bowl ad in 2022, its slowly bouncing QR code stood out in a sea of noisy spectacles, and so many viewers scanned it that the app crashed immediately. (But when every other commercial used the same tactic in 2023's championship telecast, and when thousands of other books draped themselves in swear words, the contrasting salience effect was lost.)

The best way to achieve salience is by doing something that others aren't. And the best way to do something different

Figure 6.1. Quick. Can you spot which fish is different?

is to play by rules others don't. This is the incredible creative power of constraints.

Our Preference for Contrast

Sometimes, blending in is beneficial. Blending in helps all sorts of critters avoid getting eaten by hungry predators. Soldiers and spies blend in as a matter of professional imperative. Blending in even helps you avoid getting picked on at a stand-up comedy show.

But that's not what we want as communicators. We want our advertisement, rallying cry, or safety warning to stand out from the noise and the crowd. We want to be heard and seen and understood—that's the whole point, getting from sender to receiver. This happens only when we rise above the sameness and create contrast.

Especially when we're in a busy environment, which is now every day for us, we notice what is different. Objects that are bigger or smaller, louder or quieter, lighter or darker than the rest of the context catch our eye and our minds. Scientists have run experiments where they modify photos and track participants' eyeballs with specialized cameras or where they have similar-sounding voices talk at the same time and have participants try to pick out one of them—and they all find what you'd probably expect given your own lived experience.[5] Contrast and perception have a direct, positive relationship.

We also have a natural bias toward objects and details with higher contrast. It takes less work for our brains to perceive something in sharp relief than when we have to squint and stare, such as with figure 6.2, and this

Figure 6.2. We naturally prefer higher contrast.

subconsciously translates to all sorts of good feelings. We're apt to judge images with higher contrast as more beautiful, and we're less likely to buy a product described in blurry, hard-to-distinguish text.[6] Salience is instrumental in the efficacy of our messages.

The Enemy of Contrast

Anybody who has stared at a blank canvas or silently blinking cursor knows that the expanse doesn't represent freedom but rather houses the crushing weight of the infinite. Filmmaker Orson Welles said, "The enemy of art is the absence of limitations."[7]

Without limitations, we fall into our well-worn creative grooves. We can write a slogan that sounds like everything else we've done before or craft a sermon that hits the same tired notes we've hit weekend after weekend. Psychologist

Robert Cialdini calls this the *click, whirr* phenomenon—we get into a situation, select the memory "tape" that we associate with it, then simply press play and go mindlessly *whirr* as we act out a familiar script.[8]

But a good limitation is a shock to the system. It can put up a wall that blocks business as usual and force you down a new and unfamiliar path. Maybe this detour is a side street in a different neighborhood—or maybe you're blazing a new trail altogether. Either way, the usual is the blurry background of sameness that does us little good, but the new route can lead us toward different, innovative, and maybe even brilliant new ideas. Take the road less traveled.

Adding obstacles gives you another benefit. When you limit yourself in ways others don't, you will do things others can't. Baseball players add a "doughnut" weight to their bat when they're warming up so they can swing faster when at the plate. Football players practice sprints with a parachute tugging behind them so they can run faster when being chased by a linebacker come game time. Resistance makes us stronger. Constraints make us exercise our creative muscle.

A Finite World

Finally, we have the ultimate constraint: our lives. The stoic concept of *memento mori*, Latin for "Remember that you will die," offers us an urgent reminder. The greatest artists, the most powerful rulers, and the largest characters of our age are all mortal. Our time here is finite; that's why it has meaning. Everything is fleeting.

Within the context of our finite lives, everything else snaps into place. Unlimited time and unlimited attention do not exist. We will all miss most things—we'll shuffle off this mortal coil without reading all the books we want to read, watching all the movies we mean to watch, and traveling to all the places we wish to visit. Simplicity respects this truth.

This finitude echoes downward into everything we do, including such minutiae as the limits we place on character counts, run time, and ad dimensions that we've encountered earlier in our arguments for simplicity. We don't have room or time to say everything we want to say, so we must pick and choose what works and what doesn't. We need to figure out what we want to make salient—and by definition, the answer can't be everything.

Embracing our real or self-imposed limitations pushes us to work in the art of the possible, to make things work when we think that they shouldn't. Tossing aside the illusions of infinite time, infinite resources, and infinite opportunity, we are forced to reckon with the stakes of our work—and to create ideas and messages that are fundamentally different.

Getting Salient

We'll look at three spheres for how we can use the power of constraints to help us craft more salient messages: space, time, and options. Each of these dimensions can help us put the right pressure on our work to push it out of the zone of sameness.

Limit Your Space

There's a (probably untrue) legend that notoriously succinct writer Ernest Hemingway was once challenged over lunch by

Examples of Salient and Nonsalient Messages

"Tobacco kills 1,200 people a day. Ever think about taking a day off?"
—truth

"Think. Don't smoke."
—Philip Morris

"Don't even think about parking here."
—NYC DOT

"No Parking Monday— Friday 8:00AM to 7:00PM."
—NYC DOT

"It's the economy, stupid."
—Bill Clinton

"Don't change the team in the middle of the stream."
—George H. W. Bush

his fellow writers to write a moving story in just a sentence. His tale, which handily won the bet, was "For sale, baby shoes, never worn."

And while Hemingway may not have truthfully authored that short, sorrowful story, it's held up by many as one of the best examples of constrained writing around. In just six simple words, the story includes multiple characters, a beginning, middle, and end, and a whole resulting universe of emotion. This story wouldn't pack remotely the same power if it was told using sixty, six hundred, or six thousand words. In brevity, there is clarity.

Two thousand years old and still referenced today, the ancient Roman book *Rhetorica ad Herennium* describes this as *brevitas*, using a short statement to share a much larger meaning—"the very minimum of essential words."[9]

Limitations on our space aren't a jail, they're a frame. They are a forcing mechanism that pushes us to make decisions—what stays and what goes. And when we make that decision, they showcase the beauty and value of that intention.

Though not every limitation on our space is as high-minded as literary fiction and life advice. Twitter, which is now an unfortunately notorious cesspool of bad vibes, once epitomized the value of brevitas in the social media age. For Twitter's first decade, tweets were limited to just 140 characters, a technological bottleneck resulting from its origins as an outgrowth of text messaging.

A whole new culture of communication was born from that ceiling. Users dropped now-needless adjectives and articles, shortened words by removing vowels, and pumped out staccato statements of facts and responses. Most interestingly, within these limitations, users organically created several fundamental tools of online discourse that we use today: the #hashtag for organizing related content, the @username convention for mentioning other accounts, and the retweet functionality to quote other posts. In 2017, Twitter doubled its post length to 280 characters, which users initially complained about though ultimately warmed to as a better-optimized limit on their missives. But today, as the platform is toying around with changes across the board, including character limits in the thousands, the magic pressure is gone.

When we limit how many characters, words, inches, or pixels we can use, we find creative and effective ways to make the most of them. This is the very nature of the haiku, the sonnet, and the limerick. Within the constraints of a defined vessel, we remove the burden of form and allow the full force of our minds to work on content.

Limit Your Time

Parkinson's law, a tongue-in-cheek adage coined by a twentieth-century naval historian, states that "work expands so as to fill the time available for its completion." The more time we're given to do something, the longer that task takes. Somehow, magically, every meeting scheduled for an hour happens to take an hour—even if the issue was solved in the first fifteen minutes. If we can cut down on the time we allow, it both saves that precious finite resource of ours and results in us doing our best work.

But this suggestion comes with a warning: not too much, not too little. When it comes to creative pressure, there's a Goldilocks zone where we thrive, as shown in figure 6.3. The magic is in *medium* pressure.

Once again, we all can see this from our own lives. When we get a project with a deadline way far down the line, we think that's not for us, that's a problem for our future selves. Nothing is making us do this work, so we just don't do it. Or we get started, get the first draft together, and overthink ourselves: "Maybe that idea is too out there. Maybe I should do more research. Maybe I should edit things again." With enough rope, we are apt to hang ourselves.

Then we risk the other extreme: "Shit, the client needs that presentation in an hour. No time for something new. No time for ideas. Only time for copy and paste or templates." When we have something we must do and not enough time

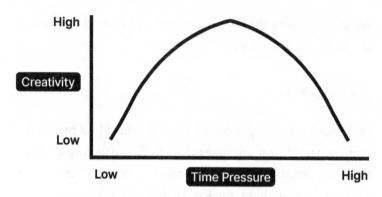

Figure 6.3. Medium pressure is the secret
to both creativity and productivity.

or resources to do it, we enter survival mode, which offers us
no oxygen for brilliance.

Beyond quality, we also face a quantity problem. When
researchers look at our rate of idea generation, they all find
the same pattern, as shown in figure 6.4.[10] We start hot, with
guns-a-blazing creativity right out of the gate. The whiteboard fills up. Sticky notes are flying. Conversations overlap
and build on each other. Then, once this burst of pent-up
ideas is over, we rapidly slow in our creativity. After about five
minutes, we've pretty much hit our limit. Ideas never fully dry
up, but the work becomes more taxing—and you're probably
better off using that energy elsewhere.

You can push against the tide and have long, tedious
meetings. Or you can harvest your creativity and move on
to the next thing. If you're unsatisfied, come back later when
your mental tank is refilled.

If the prolonged duration of your input has diminishing
returns, too much length in your output has the same problem tenfold.

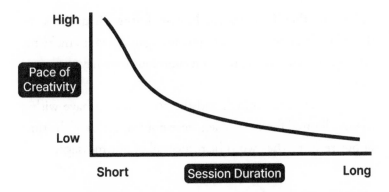

Figure 6.4. Harvest your creative energy while it is fresh, then come back and do it again.

Houses of worship are not typically known for their brevity. As a kid, I would do anything to get out of going to synagogue for four-hour services on Rosh Hashanah and Yom Kippur. (And as an adult, I feel the same dread of seemingly endless ceremonies when I join my wife's family for Easter services at their Catholic church—my gripes are nondenominational.) Regardless of religion, many of these gatherings will feature far more people zoning out instead of reaching within. But in 2018, Pope Francis, of all people, said the quiet part out loud: "How many times have we seen people sleeping during a homily, or chatting among themselves, or outside smoking a cigarette?"[11]

He saw that long, meandering homilies were ultimately selfish. They prioritized the sender, not the receiver, and certainly not the faith they were supposed to be practicing. The preachers, he said, "must be conscious that they are not doing their own thing, they are preaching." His solution: "Please, be brief . . . no more than 10 minutes, please!" While his phrasing is contemporary, the idea is not new. Five hundred years earlier, another faith leader, Martin Luther, had the same thought: "If I had my time to go over again, I would make my sermons much shorter, for I am conscious they have been too wordy."

Our days are limited, and the attention we have within them is limited further. When we're not respectful of the time of our receiver, they won't be respectful of our message.

Limit Your Options

Before the age of streaming removed shows from the shackles of a calendar, broadcast television seasons would typically clock in at twenty or more episodes each. There was time to fill, and we needed content to fill it. But production companies would still be working within the constraints of limited budgets.

To fill this calendar without breaking the bank, showrunners would often lean on what became known as the *bottle episode* format. These episodes, which feel like they take place on a ship in a bottle, are designed to cost as little as possible by using only a limited cast and limited sets—basically, just whatever the production crew already has on hand. Maybe some characters get locked in the office, stuck in an elevator, or engrossed in a dinner party.

Working within these constraints, the results of this frugality frequently end up as some of the most iconic episodes of the series, including such defining productions as *Seinfeld*'s "The Chinese Restaurant," where the characters grow increasingly frustrated waiting for a table, and *Mad Men*'s "The Suitcase," where colleagues Peggy and Don toil away in the office on professional and emotional breakthroughs late into the night. Going deep instead of wide, doing away with expensive sets and guest stars, the writers behind these shows unlock a level of creativity and excellence previously unreached.

We're in an age now when the limits are rarely technical. Still, there are perhaps no better examples of creatives bumping into, and excelling in spite of, the confines of constraints in recent history than the early days of the computer revolution. Technology improves exponentially, and at some point in the purchase or consumption of this book, you have almost certainly made use of a computer that is orders of magnitude more powerful than the supercomputers of just a few decades ago.

In the first *Super Mario Bros.* game, memory was so limited that developers needed to use the same illustration for both clouds and bushes—but the art style has now become so iconic that you can buy merchandise with it nearly forty years on. A few years later, the Super Nintendo's sound chip was limited to just sixty-four kilobyte of memory, a hundred times smaller than an MP3 you might stream today.[12] But now, music from these early video game soundtracks, composed with severe limitations and creative workarounds, is so loved that it is often played by symphonies and orchestras around the world. The dancing and bouncing GIFs we use today to react to messages and on social media are the result of programmers squeezing in images under the oppressive limits of early email providers.[13]

The limitations of processing power and memory pushed early programmers to think like another '80s icon, MacGyver, who would routinely find himself escaping tricky situations using nothing more than paper clips and duct tape. These constraints forced these creators into considering what is essential and what can be left aside. Today's technology is much closer to the infinite, and the creative pressure to make the most of each line of code has vanished into that expanse.

The best graphic designers start their work in black and white, and the best interface designers start with low-fidelity wireframes to simulate these conditions. If your idea works and your message sticks, it will still work in even the most spartan conditions. All the rest of that junk around your core idea is window dressing.

Consider, however, the opposite of such restrictions. Limiting your options can even come from the pressure of making *more* options. Go the other way: write down one hundred slogans, design one hundred banners, and develop one hundred titles for your book. Go far beyond the point where your creative groove ends. The constraint of such a high volume of output can take away your ability to do what's easy. You used up all the shortcuts in the first handful of items, and now you're forced into the creative unknown. The new, weird, different stuff is out there on the other side of normal (see figure 6.5).

We can easily get distracted by new tools, big budgets, and flashy toys and follow them down a windy path to complicated. But those paths often bring you further and further away from your core message, and they lean on the concept of more to work. By limiting yourself, by playing a different game, you can unlock messages that stand out from the sameness of everything else.

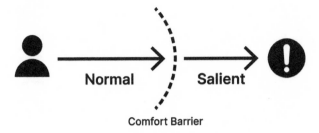

Figure 6.5. Salient is often just beyond the comfort of normal.

The Work

- What's your favorite, most-used creative tool, such as a piece of software, a turn of phrase, or a meeting format? Can you create something without it?
- Look around at your playing field. Are other people following certain language, style, or other conventions? Can you create a message that bucks these trends? What can you do differently?
- Can you describe your idea in one page? One paragraph? One sentence? One word?
- Put a minute on the clock. How many different ways can you say your message before the buzzer?
- Try something weird. What if it had to rhyme? What if you couldn't use the letter *E*? What if you could use only pictures? What if you could use only one-syllable words? What if you had to say it like Yoda?

7

Empathetic: Welcoming the Enlightened Idiot

A child of five could understand this.
Send someone to fetch a child of five.

—Groucho Marx

Captain Jean-Luc Picard has a tough job. On *Star Trek: The Next Generation*, one of my all-time favorite shows, Picard and his crew zip around the galaxy in the starship *Enterprise*, meeting aliens and saving the day, week after week in prime time.

In one of its most popular episodes, "Darmok," our protagonists run into a ship from a thorny species known as the Tamarians, who have been notoriously impossible to communicate with. The sci-fi universal translators fail, and every time these lizard-looking creatures get on a call with the *Enterprise* crew, everybody leaves frustrated that they just can't get through to each other. Tensions rise, shields go up, and trouble starts to brew.

As we learn later in the episode, the Tamarian language is exclusively based on allegories—the whole language is insider code. When the opposing captain says, "Darmok and Jalad at Tanagra," he's referencing a story in their culture of warriors teaming up to fight a common foe. When he says, "Temba, his arms wide," he's using a metaphor for generosity, and "Shaka, when the walls fell" is a tale of failure and defeat. Everything they say is a reference to something in their own cultural and historical canon. When Picard and his crew finally decipher this pattern at a crucial moment, they narrowly avoid disaster by telling their own Earth-based stories of "Gilgamesh and Enkidu, at Uruk" and "Juliet, on her balcony."

This episode makes great television, but it also shows the problem with a lot of our communication back here in the twenty-first century. Insular groups can develop their own language of references and assumptions that make it impossible for outsiders to understand, even with the help of a magic translator. Anybody who has ever sat through a corporate meeting knows it can contain an alphabet soup of acronyms and a heaping helping of jargon. This insider language can help groups work and communicate—saying "KPI" is certainly faster than "key performance indicator" fourteen times in one conversation—but it breaks down when we have to reach those outside our walls.

Effective communication is based on a shared understanding, a common ground of language, values, and experiences, between the sender and the receiver. We can achieve that level of connection only when we are earnestly empathetic with our audience.

Why Empathy Matters

We can avoid the fate of a fictional phaser beam or a real-life clunky sales call by harnessing the power of empathy and welcoming a character we'll call the *Enlightened Idiot*.

Who is the Enlightened Idiot? It's not a single person or a separate group of people. The Enlightened Idiot is all of us when we step outside our bubbles.

The word *idiot* sounds rough, and indeed, people often use it today as an insult—but here we mean it with love. If you trace back to the ancient Greek origins of the word, it used to mean "common man," not somebody of low intelligence. As for the use of *enlightened*, that's defined as being free of misinformation and of bias. The Enlightened Idiot is aspirational.

The Enlightened Idiot is a stand-in for everybody else. They are not in the room, and they are not in your head. They are somebody who doesn't know as much about what you're saying—and frankly, they probably don't care as much about what you're saying as you do. They embody your boss's busy aloofness and your kindergartner's gentle ignorance. In other words, they're your audience.

We're all Enlightened Idiots sometimes, just like we're all experts sometimes. If you're Jill, a brilliant scientist holding a TED Talk on your latest advances in genomics, it helps to bring in Jack from the accounting department for your rehearsals to see if he gets it. If you're Jack, the all-star CPA, planning to hold a webinar on how university faculty should be organizing their expense reports, bringing in Jill to review a dry run will be far more insightful than his other spreadsheet-minded colleagues. It doesn't matter that they both have advanced degrees; both Jack and Jill can be Enlightened Idiots.

Outsiders expose our preconceived notions, bring fresh ideas, and can shake us out of our bubble of ignorance. They see things we can't, and they know things we don't. Their welcomed perspective enlightens the rest of us.

You Are Not the Audience

Here's a hard pill to swallow: you are not the receiver. Your life is not the same as theirs, and what you want is not the same as what they want. You have knowledge, experience, and values that they don't have—and vice versa.

In just over a decade, social media platforms such as Facebook and LinkedIn did something that had never been done before in the history of humankind. Everybody everywhere is now connected to each other. The town square is now the size of the planet, and the diverse marketplace of ideas is flourishing inside it.

Not so fast—a growing body of research shows that instead of tapping into the global debate, we've created our own echo chambers. A 2015 study of Facebook relationships found that, on average, just 20 percent of liberals' friends on the platform are conservative, and only 18 percent of conservatives' friends are liberal.[1] As TikTok has popularized the algorithmic "For You" feed model, this isolation has gone further. Other studies have shown that the more we use these social media echo chambers, the more likely we are to falsely believe that other people share not just our politics but also our personality traits and social motivations.[2] Even when we theoretically have access to everybody, we have a hard time grappling with the fact that our experiences, attitudes, and abilities are not universal.

These examples highlight what psychologists call the *false-consensus effect*. In short, we assume that other people share the same opinions and attributes as us and that we are basically representative of what is popular, right, and normal. Except usually, we're wrong.

In 1977, researchers Lee Ross, David Greene, and Pamela House first defined this concept in a series of foundational studies, each exhibiting that we're pretty bad at intuitively guessing what other people will think and do.[3] Participants tended to think that more people would side with their own choices when asked about contesting speeding tickets, agreeing to be recorded in an ad for a local supermarket, and choosing which type of homework assignment for a class. In another study, participants believed that the others in the study were more likely to agree with them about their preference for a type of bread or foreign film, that they subscribe to the same magazines, or even that they agree on the odds that we'll make contact with aliens than was the norm.[4]

In a more recent example of our penchant for bad assumptions, researchers asked participants if a reasonable person would hand over their unlocked phone to experimenters, and only 28 percent said they would.[5] Most of us would likely agree that's bonkers—our finances, messages, and photos are all on there. But when these same participants were asked to do just that, more than 97 percent complied. Yet again, we hardly know ourselves, and we barely know others, living as in figure 7.1.

There are a number of reasons we goof up on this so often. We are likely to hang out and work with people who are a lot like us, with similar socioeconomic or educational backgrounds. As a result, the birds of a feather we're regularly exposed to likely lead similar lives and have similar views. This tendency is known as *homophily*, and we see it occur across demographic traits like age and gender but also in terms of occupations and interests. While this clustering behavior can certainly be intentional, it more often benignly results from other upstream factors, such as geography or family dynamics. Either way, we have to be aware of how this filter paints our perceptions.

Then we need to consider the person we spend the *most* time with—ourselves. We're most familiar with what we think and do, and we are apt to use that to fill in the blanks when we're faced with ambiguity and uncertainty. Furthermore, we often just plain ol' want our opinions and behaviors to be the correct ones, and we approach the world around us with a corresponding bias. Thinking we're right takes less cognitive work than believing otherwise. As Montesquieu wrote, "If triangles had a god, they would give him three sides."

We're all biased, and we have to accept that reality to address it. Our insider perspectives and knowledge, if not accounted for, will prevent us from getting our message across. We need to get out of our own way.

Figure 7.1. We live in our bubbles.

Bubbles Must Be Busted

The stubborn truth is that corporate America is still almost a complete monoculture, dominated by middle- and upper-income, college-educated, white men. To wit, 61 percent of C-suite executives are white men, and only six companies in the entire Fortune 500 have Black CEOs.[6] Women get promoted less and leave the workforce more—and nearly a third of the time, a woman in an engineering or technical role will literally find herself to be the only woman in the room. Insiders, insiders, insiders.

We're all worse off for this echo chamber. When we don't have diverse views in the room deciding how we communicate, what results are ghastly ads featuring the likes of Ashton Kutcher in brownface and a cringey Bollywood accent promoting Popchips or a photoshoot by H&M of a young Black boy modeling a sweatshirt reading "Coolest Monkey in the Jungle." Hundreds of people saw both of those now-notoriously tone-deaf productions before they were released, and nobody pumped the brakes. If you have a team that looks like the world instead of looking like each other, this kind of disaster just doesn't happen.

Beyond the moral argument, diversity of teams is just plain good business every way you slice it. More diverse companies are proven to be more innovative, productive, and profitable. Three out of four employees prefer to work on inclusive teams.[7] And when we look at the goal of most business communication, sparking growth, the benefits of diversity are even starker. The most diverse companies are 45 percent likelier to win market share and even 70 percent more likely to capture new markets altogether.[8] Busting your bubble pays off handsomely—and staying in it comes at a price.

The mechanism through which diversity gives us these benefits is the same one that makes the instructions about subtraction so effective when we discussed focus in chapter 5: the availability bias. Having a wider range of views and experiences readily available to us, within easy reach, means that we are more likely to pick them up and use them. If instead, we stay in a world where everybody looks, acts, and thinks the same as we do, we're hurting ourselves and our audience.

Getting Empathetic

Building empathy into our communications requires that we get out of our own space and occupy the perspective of our receiver. We can achieve this by engaging with our audience and building in diverse perspectives, as well as shifting our internal models to drive us away from dangerous assumptions and toward authentic connection.

Test Your Message on Other People

You can easily convince yourself that you make sense. You have lots of experience listening to the voice in your head and figuring out what it's saying. You're really convincing because you're already convinced.

Everybody else doesn't have this insider's edge when it comes to deciphering your ideas. Until you break your message out of your bubble and take it out into the world, you have no idea if you're actually saying what you mean to say.

Examples of Empathetic and Nonempathetic Messages

"You only have to floss the teeth you want to keep."
  —My dentist

"You should floss to prevent plaque buildup below the gumline."
  —My old dentist

"Are you better off today than you were four years ago?"
  —Ronald Reagan

"A tested and trustworthy team."
  —Jimmy Carter

"When it absolutely, positively, has to be there overnight."
  —FedEx

"What can brown do for you?"
  —UPS

This is where we get to the most obvious and most overlooked tool in our empathy kit: testing your message on other people.

Testing your message on others is the most no-brainer tactic in this entire book, yet it will likely be the most ignored. We're often afraid of getting feedback because the feedback might be bad. And negative feedback is inherently uncomfortable. But we must push past that discomfort.

A whole industry is built around this function. Marketing research firms and public opinion pollsters employ thousands of people to facilitate focus groups and send surveys. Maybe you've even been on the receiving end yourself. No offense to my many friends who work in this field, but most of us don't need all of that.

We can start small. Pull an Enlightened Idiot into the room from another part of the office. Send an email to a few friends that fit your target and ask for their feedback. Run an inexpensive online survey, or even try out a small test advertising campaign using any of the dozens of online tools to get you feedback for pennies. Doing just this limited, unscientific research will put you ahead of everybody else who is too afraid to ask.

As we said in chapter 5, "Done is king." Simply bringing in a few people (who resemble your audience) into the conversation is already more than what others are doing. You might remember from math class that if you do it right, you don't actually need to survey a ton of people to draw conclusions about large groups. Gallup, one of the leading polling companies in the United States, routinely delivers insights about the country's 330 million people based on polls conducted with just one thousand respondents.[9] If you're testing your next sales pitch, a handful of Enlightened Idiots is all you need.

The legendary startup accelerator Y Combinator has helped propel companies like Airbnb, Reddit, and Dropbox into multibillion dollar empires. Each year, hundreds of entrepreneurs compete tooth and nail for a chance to join the program. Paul Graham, cofounder of Y Combinator, writes an influential blog that routinely shapes the conversation in tech and is religiously studied by those applicants. What's his number one advice for getting in? "Explain what you've learned from users." He continues, "That tests a lot of things: whether you're paying attention to users, how well you understand them, and even how much they need what you're making."[10]

A company that doesn't communicate with its users is dead in the water, and a communicator who doesn't talk to their audience is just as helpless.

A word of warning when you're doing this research: testing and using focus groups can tell you if something is working or not, but they can't tell you *where* to go. People don't know what they want—as the story goes, they'd more likely ask for faster horses than automobiles. Truthfully, we don't want their advice or their opinion so much as their response. Look at them as a compass, not a tour guide.

Harness the Magic of Outsiders

Google's founders saw that ideas originating from the rank-and-file staff had a higher success rate than those that came from the top down. Wilbur and Orville Wright were amateur tinkerers and bike shop owners, but they beat out engineers and academics in the race for the sky. Hungarian-born Katalin Karikó, daughter of a butcher and child of a home without running water or a refrigerator, was rejected time and again by her establishment colleagues—but her lonely work on mRNA technology led to the COVID-19 vaccines that have saved millions of lives.[11]

Whether an outsider by occupation, education, or biography, time and again, outsiders benefit from something that insiders don't: they don't know what they're not supposed to do. They have what Zen Buddhists call *shoshin*, a beginner's mind. Beginners are open and eager, looking to learn and unimpeded by the burden of preconceptions. Experience helps us grow, but it can also calcify us in our ways of doing and thinking, making us blind to everything else. At worst, we become cherry-picking pattern matchers, accepting what confirms our approach and disregarding views and evidence that might challenge it. Beginners and outsiders don't bear this suffocating weight of brain clutter.

Renowned design firm IDEO describes those with a wide, outside view as *cross-pollinators*, people who can draw "associations and connections between seemingly unrelated ideas or concepts to break new ground."[12] Cross-pollinators bring different aspects and ideas together in ways that siloed insiders can't easily see. They take concepts from one area and bring them to bear in another, completely different space. These simmering stews of creativity and connection brought forth by outsiders are the sources of some of our greatest innovations and movements.

Don't Assume Anything

There's a hokey saying about assumptions plastered on a zillion novelty mugs that goes something like this: "When you assume, you make an *ass* out of *u* and *me*."

The only assumption any sender should make is that our receivers are doing *just fine*. They didn't wake up today eager to hear your sales pitch or safety warning. They didn't have "watch commercials" or "click social media ads" on their agenda today. They weren't planning to read your press release or visit your website. They care about a lot of things—but the odds are good that your message isn't one of them.

When we assume otherwise—that our receiver has the ability and motivation to seek out and analyze our message— sometimes we're right, but far more often we're wrong. The upside benefit of being right is mostly marginal and is greatly overshadowed by the downside risk of being wrong and failing to connect altogether. If instead, we humbly operate under the prevailing expectation of ignorance or apathy, we can better design messaging that fits into their lives.

We need to understand that our common knowledge isn't always so common. We all know lots of things that others don't, and we have an awful habit of taking our knowledge as a given. Baseball fans assume everybody knows where the shortstop plays, and geologists assume that everybody knows the general gist of plate tectonics. But if you've never watched a ballgame or taken a science class, these basics will be foreign concepts.

The sin of assumption manifests most often in messages that start with "Don't forget . . ." or "Remember to . . ." These crutches are simultaneously lazy and arrogant. You can't forget something you never knew. And while we all forget (with these stupid brains and all), if somebody needs to be reminded to remember something, you probably didn't do a great job getting it through to them in the first place. If you drop these assumptions and just get to it, your message will almost always be more potent.

Designers have long known of a phenomenon called *desire lines*, which you've seen if you've ever cut across a field on a well-worn informal path or used a treadmill as a clothes hanger (see figure 7.2). Despite what the builders of that park or treadmill intended, users wanted to do something different with the design and created their own way to do so. When Michigan State University was designing its campus, it left it unpaved. After students formed their own network of paths through thousands of footfalls, the planners turned around and paved these desire lines. Urban advocate Jane Jacobs described the bottom-up power of these types of lines, "There is no logic that can be superimposed on the city; people make it, and it is to them . . . that we must fit our plans."[13]

Our audience will tell us where they want to go; we just have to listen. Learning from the Enlightened Idiot as

Figure 7.2. Desire lines tell us where people want to go.

you develop and test your messages will help you find these paths.

Talk Like a Human to a Human

A few years ago, I was at dinner with some friends, and one of them was working at a company whose name was currently splashed across the news due to a rather unfortunate product design flaw. Some pretty damning footage of a major defect was spreading around on social media, and talking heads on the business shows were sternly debating about what this scandal meant for the company's future. Given all this gruesome news, somebody across the table asked this friend how things were going at work. The response, sent down from corporate overlords to be parroted verbatim by all staff: "It's unfortunate that these events occurred, and . . ."

Everybody broke out laughing. We all felt like we were sitting down to eat with a press release. Humans simply don't speak that way. You've never used "It's unfortunate . . ." to lead a sentence in your life unless you're trying to wordsmith something polite or lawyers are breathing down your neck to deny any liability. Instead, we speak like a human: "It sucks."

In the United Kingdom in 2018, pretty much the worst thing that could happen did happen to fried-chicken juggernaut KFC: it ran out of chicken. Due to an unfortunate highway accident involving its distributor and a series of other logistics failures, three-quarters of the restaurant's nine hundred locations in the country had to temporarily close as it ran out of its namesake product. It was a nightmare.[14]

The traditional public relations handbook would call for a formal press release, and a stiff man in a suit would stand in front of some microphones, explain the situation, and apologize for any "inconvenience." But that's how a business speaks, not how a person does. Instead, KFC took out full-page ads in the United Kingdom's top newspapers with a simple, honest graphic: its iconic red and white bucket but with "FCK" written across the front. In the text below, it shared more human honesty: "We're sorry. A chicken restaurant without any chicken. It's not ideal." In just one ad, using refreshingly natural language, it apologized for its "hell of a week" and flipped the media narrative on its head.

If you need help figuring out how to talk like a human, well, *talk to a human.* Try leaning over to a colleague or calling up your friend and telling them what you want to say. If you can say your message with a straight face and not sound like you're doing voice-over work, you're good. If you feel uncomfortable saying what you need to say in conversation, then you need to go back and workshop it.

Writing about writing, prolific author and marketer Seth Godin said, "No one ever gets talker's block."[15] We talk every day, and we never get stuck—but writer's block is a problem for many. Why? He answers, "We get better at talking precisely because we talk." He goes on to expand on the virtue of daily practice, which is a great habit to improve your work, though we can use this insight as a shortcut.

If your message is stiff and just won't shake loose the burdensome confines of business-speak, take it off the page and talk it out. Talk to yourself in the shower, talk to your spouse over breakfast, or, best yet, talk to somebody who's close to your audience. By virtue of thousands of daily reps, your talking muscle is probably a lot stronger than your writing one, so use it.

The Work

- What does the receiver know that you don't? What questions can they answer better than you?
- What assumption are you most sure about? What would it mean if you're wrong about that?
- What word or idea in your message do you think will be the least understood? Can you replace it with something simpler?
- What does your message sound like to somebody with bad intentions or somebody who won't give you the benefit of the doubt? How does it look in the worst possible light?
- How would you say this message to your best friend over dinner?

8

Minimal:
Say Shit without
the Bullshit

Art is the elimination of the unnecessary.

—Pablo Picasso

On June 16, 2015, Donald Trump descended a gilded esca-
lator in the lobby of his namesake tower and announced
his candidacy for president of the United States. His speech
and run quickly became a punchline for late-night comedians
and serious political pundits alike.

It's hard to remember in hindsight, but before Trump's
announcement, members of the Republican Party were calling the field of seventeen candidates, which included popular
governors, experienced senators, and respected outsiders, the

"deepest and strongest" they had ever seen.[1] The early front-runner, Jeb Bush, was the brother of the last Republican president and son of the previous one. Pundits fawned over other favorites—Senators Marco Rubio, a rising star from Florida, and Ted Cruz, a bomb-throwing partisan from Texas—as potentially helping the party make new demographic inroads. You can't really blame the insiders for thinking this tabloid-creature reality star was going nowhere fast.

But the whole race was changed by one line at the end of Trump's speech: "I will bring it back bigger and better and stronger than ever before, and we will make America great again."

Those final four words became his straightforward campaign slogan from start to finish. It was immortalized on garish red hats and as a hashtagged acronym "#MAGA" on millions of Twitter profiles.

Those words were so powerful because they gave voters a simple answer to the question "Why do you support that guy?" They'd reply that Trump will "make America great again." It's a full sentence. And while his catchphrase is loaded with heavy racial and historical baggage, it's a vehicle compact enough to fit on those hats and in your brain without needing further explanation.

Bush didn't get this. His infamous logo was "Jeb!" and his hashtag, "#AllInForJeb." What are we supposed to do with this?

Rubio didn't get this. His slogan was "A New American Century." What on earth does that mean?

Cruz didn't get this. His slogan was "Together, we will win." Okay, but win what? How? Why?

After Trump sealed the nomination, he faced off against Hillary Clinton in November's general election. One of the most famous people, let alone politicians, in the world, with a résumé that includes stints as secretary of state, United States senator, and first lady, Clinton was as formidable a challenger as they come. But while she had the most experienced team in the business, her campaign struggled to articulate a simple reason for her candidacy. At different points, the Clinton campaign used the following slogans: "Stronger together," "I'm with her," "Fighting for us," and "Love trumps hate." All of these are nice, short phrases that look good enough on a yard sign—but they're squishy and shapeless messages when held up to internal and external interrogation.

Why are you voting for your candidate? For all the chaos of the campaign that followed, and the controversial administration that sprung from it, Trump did one thing right on that first day that his opponents never did: he gave supporters an easy answer.

On the other end of the political spectrum, the establishment was rocked again just two years after Trump took office.

Representing the diverse communities of Queens and the Bronx since 1999, Congressman Joe Crowley was widely viewed as one of the most powerful figures in New York—and an odds-on favorite to become a future Speaker of the House. Year after year, Crowley faced little to no competition for his seat, cruising to victory in ten straight elections. As chairman of the Queens County Democratic Party, he was as influential a kingmaker as you could find in modern American politics.

Good money would say his eleventh run for Congress would go his way.

But 2018 was no ordinary election year, and all across the country, energized Democratic activists were beginning to challenge establishment politicians whom they saw as lacking. In New York, a young candidate from the Bronx named Alexandria Ocasio-Cortez was among this cohort as she bid to unseat Crowley—giving him his first primary challenge since 2004.

We're lucky to get an intimate glimpse at Ocasio-Cortez's campaign in the 2019 documentary *Knock Down the House*.[2] In it, we see her sitting on a couch, taking a sip of coffee, and explaining the advantage in perspective and messaging that was powering her insurgent campaign.

Holding up a glossy campaign mailer from Crowley with a large, closely cropped photo of his face on the cover, she says, "So look at this thing. Everybody in the district got this Victoria's Secret catalog of my opponent."

Ocasio-Cortez reaches for her own postcard. "I mean, I'm not trying to gas myself up or brag or anything, but this is the difference between an *organizer* and a *strategist*."

We see the two pieces of marketing material side by side now: Crowley's large face and logo on the left, Ocasio-Cortez's purple and white piece on the right. Pointing at hers, moving from her name to a headline with voting info, she asks, "What am I trying to get people to do? Two things, I want them to know my name, and I want them to know that they need to vote."

Rhetorically, she continues, "Okay, vote for her. Why?" and then flips the card over to reveal half a dozen no-nonsense bullets. "End the war on drugs. 100 percent renewable energy. Tuition-free public college."

Shifting gears, Ocasio-Cortez pulls Crowley's mailer back into the frame and says, "This is how a strategist does it. Where's the primary date on this? When you first see it, when you first pull this out of your mailbox?" It's not there. She reads what is: "Taking on Donald Trump in Washington. Delivering for Queens and the Bronx." Exasperated, she adds, "*Deliver* is insider talk."

The candidate continues the tour inside the "big, beautiful spread," and a date is still nowhere to be found. Her comparison concludes, "There is nothing about the path forward here. 'Trump' three times, commitments zero times."

More communications know-how is on display in this one-minute clip than many political and business leaders exhibit in their whole careers. Most buyers, voters, and donors just need it straight—who are you, what do you want, and why should I care?

The primary date that was so elusive on Crowley's mailer was June 26, 2018. When polls closed that night, the city and the country were shocked. Ocasio-Cortez defeated the incumbent with nearly 57 percent of the vote, becoming a national sensation in the process.

Why Minimal Matters

The last of our five principles is *minimal*, and that placement is deliberate. Minimal is about having everything you need— but only what you need. This determination can come only after we make sure that our communication is beneficial, focused, salient, and empathetic. Those conditions are all necessary before we can know what is essential and what is not.

Brevity is a common trait of minimal messages, but it's not the definition. Most lifestyle minimalists don't actually advocate for an absolute lack of possessions; instead they say to embrace what matters while stripping away what doesn't. Marie Kondo, who we first saw in chapter 2, actually separates herself further from the idea of spartan austerity with her KonMari method, which "encourages living among items you truly cherish."[3]

Instead, we put on our engineering hats and treat minimal messaging as the design challenge that it is. We're focused on minimizing friction by avoiding off-ramps and ensuring structural integrity. Off-ramps are ways in which our message gets distracted or diluted. Structurally sound messages can hold up to the challenges of our environment.

Off-Ramps

No matter which side of the political divide you land on, both of the political figures at the top of our chapter communicate in a similar way: they said shit without the bullshit. Tossing all the usual crap out the window and embracing straight-to-the-point messages have catapulted them to the most influential heights of political power. And this same strategy has launched brands and leaders across industries to the top of their respective arenas.

Bullshit is an off-ramp. Unnecessarily complicated language or words and terms without clear meanings become opportunities for the receiver to pull off and check out, as illustrated in figure 8.1. The voters in our stories above saw the same old rhetoric from candidates and disconnected. Website visitors that read large but empty words such as *revolutionary, superior,* or *responsible* have their eyes glaze over and click back for something else.

Cracking open the thesaurus for a tour de force of Scrabble-worthy jargon isn't going to wow the receiver into your arms. Adding a bucket of syllables doesn't mean you win a battle of wits and, as the victor, you'll have earned the purchase, vote, donation, or whatever else it was you were hoping for. Instead, you're much more likely to make yourself look like a dummy.

Researchers at Princeton University prepared two sets of sample grad school application essays: one control set and one where they turned up the complexity dial by swapping out words for longer synonyms.[4] Judges were then asked if they would accept the hypothetical applicant, how confident they were in that decision, and then ultimately to rate the difficulty of the passage.

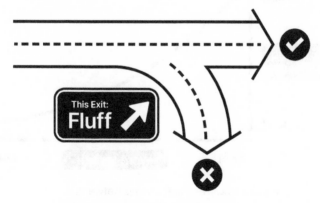

Figure 8.1. Don't give your receivers an off-ramp from your message.

Smarter students have larger vocabularies and make better applicants, right? Nope. The bigger the words, the harder it was to read, and the less likely that the judges accepted the applicant, as shown in figure 8.2. The results were clear, unlike the dense essays, as they explained: "Simple texts were given higher ratings than moderately complex texts, which were, in turn, given better ratings than highly complex texts."

When the same team ran the experiment in reverse, this time simplifying a dense essay into a clearer one, the results held true. Judges consistently rated the authors of simpler works as more intelligent and those of more complex essays as less intelligent. Even when they tested professional translations of seventeenth-century French philosopher René Descartes, participants held the same opinion: the simpler author was smarter, and the complicated one sounded dumber.

Big words are less fluent. When something is harder to read, see, or understand, that struggle turns into distrust and dislike. When we use big words to cover small ideas, we're

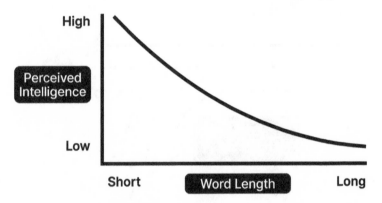

Figure 8.2. The relationship between word length and perceived intelligence.

increasing friction and turning off the people we're trying to reach, and in the process making that off-ramp look awfully tempting.

Structural Integrity

Communication works only when you use language that meets the following basic criteria:

+ The sender understands it.
+ The receiver understands it.

If both ends of the equation understand the language that makes up your message, then you're cooking. If they don't, then you've failed right at the get-go. It doesn't matter how good of a commercial you've crafted, if it's in Italian or if its dialogue is ripped straight from a medical dictionary, I can't understand it. If it's full of industry buzzwords or acronyms, like in figure 8.3, you've lost me. When a message doesn't pass this test, it's not structurally sound—it collapses.

The challenge is that, for most of us, communication doesn't have to be scientific jargon or in a foreign language to be unreadable. According to the US Department of Education, 21 percent of American adults are either barely literate or functionally illiterate, and we get beat in literacy stats by dozens of other nations when you look at cross-border comparisons. In particular, a history of inequity has disproportionately hurt minority populations in this metric.[5] As a matter of morals, and of public policy, we can and should do better.

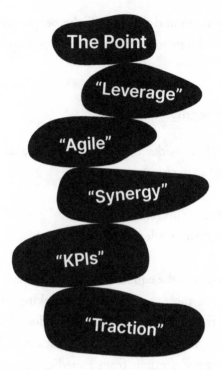

Figure 8.3. Each piece of jargon is another point of failure.

But we have to play it as it lies. We must face the reality that the costs add up steeply with every ten-dollar word we use. You can push the boundaries, and people will pick up a few words here and there from context clues, but if you step too far, you'll fall off the reading comprehension cliff.

When Boomerang, an email application, analyzed millions of conversations, it found that emails written at a college reading level had, by far, the worst response rate.[6] The ones that had the best response rate? Written at a third-grade level.

The speech mentioned at the start of this chapter? A fourth-grade level.

Language changes and grows over time, and the pace of this change is accelerating each year as more and more of us connect and exchange ideas on a global scale. In one recent month, the *Oxford English Dictionary* added or updated over 1,500 words—which works out to a new definition every twenty-nine minutes.[7] The ground keeps shifting, and we must make sure we're building our message on accessible, solid foundations for it to work.

Complex systems fail because they have multiple points of possible failure, and complex messages fall apart the same way. Nobel laureate Daniel Kahneman and his longtime collaborator Amos Tversky explain: "A complex system, such as a nuclear reactor or the human body, will malfunction if any of its essential components fails. Even when the likelihood of failure in each component is slight, the probability of an overall failure can be high if many components are involved."[8]

Each additional component in a message is another source of possible failure, or at least a point of friction. Don't make your receiver work for it—because they won't.

When famed physicist Stephen Hawking wrote his blockbuster book *A Brief History of Time*, his publisher warned that each equation included in the text would halve the sales.[9] Despite covering the "complete understanding of the universe," he limited the text to just one equation, "$e = mc^2$." If he can cover the big bang and black holes with just one bit of jargon, you can cut out complexity too.

Examples of Minimal and Nonminimal Messages

"Eat food. Mostly plants. Not too much."
—Michael Pollan

"Follow a healthy eating pattern across a lifespan."
—US Department of Health and Human Services

"Give me liberty or give me death."
—Patrick Henry

"Address yourselves to the King and the two Houses of Parliament. Let your representations be decent and firm, and principally directed to obtain a solid American Constitution; such as we can accept with safety, and Great-Britain can grant with dignity."
—Samuel Seabury

"Loose lips sink ships."
—War Advertising Council

"Don't discuss troop movements, ship sailings, war equipment."
—United States Office of War Information

Getting Minimal

Developing minimal messages requires us to consider first principles, what Aristotle called "the first basis from which a thing is known."[10] If we break what we want to say into its basic building blocks, we can assemble a message that hits all the necessary notes without getting distracted by things that don't serve our mission. We'll start with analyzing the elements of positioning, then examine the language we use to articulate it, and finally end with considering how that message looks in the world.

Answer the "Why?"

People like to have reasons for doing the things they do. Even when their decisions are emotional or irrational, people like to think they have a logical reason for why they buy what they buy, vote for who they vote for, and donate to who they donate to.

So give it to them.

The most valuable gift you can give your audience is a reason to choose you that they can parrot back to themselves and others. It puts their mind at ease and gives them an easy answer when quizzed by others. It gives people something to hold on to.

Why did you vote for Trump? Well, he was going to make America great again. Why did you vote for Obama? He was a change we could believe in.

Why did I start flossing? Because my dentist said you only have to floss the teeth you want to keep. Why do you vacation at Disney World? Because it's the happiest place on earth.

Make it easy for somebody to feel good about choosing you, and people will feel better about choosing you.

In brand marketing, the art of figuring out this answer is called *positioning*, and you can begin to find yours by answering three basic questions:

- Who is your stuff for?
- What problem do they have that you solve?
- Why are you better than all the other ways to solve that problem?

Like everything else here, these questions are simple but the answers are hard. Brand consultants get paid big money to ask these questions to organizations every day—and you'd be amazed by how many people can't answer them about themselves and their businesses. You can't be for everybody. You can't solve every problem. And you can't be the best at everything.

Asking yourself these questions defines where you are positioned in the market, and thus where you are in the mind of the receiver. This building block keeps you focused and on the right path as you move forward.

Start from the Ground Up

If you want to speak and be heard, one of the best ways is to put yourself in a box. Try to say your idea using only the ten hundred most used words. When you try it and make it work, you will understand how to explain what you mean more simply. After you crack that, then you can add in the harder words.

What the hell did I mean by "ten hundred" words? Well, ten hundred is one thousand, which is the limiting factor in that paragraph above. If that passage seems a little weird, it's because I wrote it using only words from the one thousand most commonly used in English. When I was typing it out,

I wanted to use lots of words that threw up red flags: *limit*, *mastered*, and *complicated* didn't make the cut.

Randall Munroe, the creator of the popular and long-running webcomic *xkcd*, wrote a whole book this way titled *Thing Explainer*.[11] Limiting himself to only the thousand most common words in the English language, he explains, humorously but accurately, all sorts of technical subjects—from cameras and microwaves to atomic bombs, or, to put it in his simplified language, "picture takers," "food-heating radio boxes," and "machines for burning cities." Scientist Peter Gleick, in his review of the book, gave this project high praise, writing, "There is a page about the color of light that is one of the best explainers about this hard idea that I've ever read. My teachers at school could have learned a thing or two about teaching from this."

As it turns out, those one thousand words make up 75 percent of all written English—a language with over 170,000 of them.[12] If you think that concentration is intense, our usage is even more top-weighted than that: the top hundred words make up 50 percent of English, and the top ten words (*the, be, to, of, and, a, in, that, have, I*) account for a full 25 percent of our language as it's used. English and all other languages follow a pattern called Zipf's law, which states the frequency of a word is inversely proportional to its rank: the most common word in English (*the*) shows up about one-tenth of the time in usage, the second most common (*be*) appears one-twentieth of the time, and so on.

The calculation doesn't matter much for our purposes, but the conclusion does: you can cover a lot of ground using just the most popular words. And you'll build a much sturdier message by doing so.

Start with the simplest possible language and go from there. Don't reach for the big ones unless you absolutely have to—they'll pack more punch when you use them sparingly. But when in doubt, clear beats clever.

Cut the Fluff

About half of all writing advice boils down to the same idea: cut out all the crap you don't need.

In a 1946 essay, George Orwell laid out six rules for writing, three of which were "Never use a long word where a short one will do," "If it is possible to cut a word out, always cut it out," and "Never use a foreign phrase, a scientific word or a jargon word if you can think of an everyday English equivalent."[13]

Another frequently quoted passage on writing comes from William Strunk Jr. and E. B. White's *The Elements of Style*, under the heading "Omit needless words":

> Vigorous writing is concise. A sentence should contain no unnecessary words, a paragraph no unnecessary sentences, for the same reason that a drawing should have no unnecessary lines and a machine no unnecessary parts. This requires not that the writer make all his sentences short, or that he avoid all detail and treat his subjects only in outline, but that every word tell.[14]

These "unnecessary words" are fodder for our mental spam filter—they're off-ramps.

When dollars and cents come into this, people get it. Next time you try to check out while shopping online, take a look around the page. All the buttons that might lead you away from the virtual cash register are gone. You can't click back to the home page, blog, or categories section. All you can do, unless you get out of there by clicking back or closing your browser, is enter your card number and complete the sale. Every pixel on that page is serving its goal. Effective communication does the same.

Benjamin Dreyer, as copy chief at Random House, has read and edited more words than just about anybody else alive. In his own book, *Dreyer's English*, he dedicates a whole chapter to what he dubs "trimmables," redundant words that can be cut almost every time they appear. Here's a sample, with the trimmables in italics:

- *Added* bonus
- Crisis *situation*
- *Fiction* novel
- Plan *ahead*
- *Unsolved* mystery[15]

In my experience as a marketer, I can add one more big one: *help*. The new face wash doesn't help make you look younger; it makes you look younger. The to-do app doesn't help you be more productive; it makes you more productive. People don't want products that help them—they want products that work. Quit the hedging, and your offer will be much clearer. (Just be prepared to go to bat when your lawyers try pushing back the other way.)

Much of what we say and write is focused on reaching a goal framed as a minimum—hitting a word count, filling a column, or adding a caption. In that pursuit, we call in this type of fluff. But when we flip the script and consciously fight against the desire for more, we end up with punchier, better messages. Usability researchers have found that concise writing can improve the effectiveness of our messages by as much as 58 percent.[16] Trimming the excess is the single biggest improvement you can make.

Minimal communication isn't about removing everything and stripping down your message to the fewest number of words. But it does require us to once again understand the core, zero-sum trade-off: everything we add means that everything else is less important. Every word must earn its keep.

If there is no quiet, there can be no loud. We need to remove the noise for the signal to shine through. If we don't, we risk a response like the well-worn meme in figure 8.4.

Speak to One Person, Not a Crowd

Every message is one-to-one. It doesn't matter if a politician is on stage at a rally speaking to five thousand people or a Super Bowl commercial is broadcasting to 100 million. On the level at which you are actually connecting, there is always only one sender and one receiver.

Speaking to a crowd doesn't work because crowds don't exist. Though we can act as groups, and we've built structures and communities that allow us to collectively do things that we can't do by ourselves, we're still the only ones

Figure 8.4. I ain't reading all that.
Credit: Twitter account @nocontextdms for source,
author for illustration

living in our heads. Every product you've ever bought and every vote you've ever cast has been because of the message that you individually received and processed that led to that decision.

This is why messaging that speaks to a vague, faceless notion of a group doesn't land. Ads that address us as "readers," "New Yorkers," "cat owners," or, worse yet, "some of you" can easily just whiz by without us giving them a moment's notice.

The receiver is never "some of you"—they're just "you." I can be in a group, but I am not *the* group.

Influencers across a range of platforms have discovered that social media posts that start with broad greetings such as "Folks," "Hey guys," or "Everybody" feel flatter and less intimate than content that is more direct and personal. Many of the best TikToks feel like a friend giving you a FaceTime call, and some of the most viral tweets feel like a text message. As you've seen in your own inbox, emails with personalized subject lines are 26 percent more likely to be clicked and read than broadcast ones.[17]

Marketing agencies with big budgets will develop tools for this practice called *personas*, fictionalized ideal customers with a whole biographical sketch written out on a slide. That's great if you can do it, but you can immediately get halfway there a lot faster and a lot cheaper. Print out a photo and put it on your desk, or even just take a sticky note, doodle a little stick figure, and slap it on your monitor. Look at it. That's who you are writing to, that's who you are speaking to. We communicate with individuals, not the masses.

Think Visually

About half of our brain is devoted, in some way, to processing what comes in through our eyes.[18] Most of our communication—be it a website, social media post, print ad, email, text message, or memo—is visual, even if what you're looking at is words. Cleaning up how your message literally looks is a vital (and too often overlooked) part of getting your ideas across.

By using specialized tools full of precise sensors and cameras, or even just the webcam built into a laptop or smartphone, designers and researchers can track where those eyes of ours are pointing and how we use websites and apps.[19] The results are uniform: we don't really read most of what's shown on the screen.

Here's how we generally consume information on a screen:

+ We start at the top left and move down, scanning from left to right, first at the top and then farther down the screen, like the letter *F*. (In right-to-left languages, such as Arabic or Hebrew, the effect is flipped.)

+ We jump to words and sections that stand out visually, such as links, bolded sections, and bulleted lists (like this one).

+ We look for relevant words, or at least those shaped like they should be, to the task at hand, such as addresses, names, phone numbers, or prices.

+ We jump headlines and subheadings looking for what's interesting, which researchers call the *layer cake* pattern.

Only when we're really motivated do we do what we might think of as the default mode: reading the whole text of a page from top to bottom. We're so inundated by the fire hose of information that's shot at us every day that we've all become skimmers, like in figure 8.5.

Longtime political reporters Jim VandeHei, Mike Allen, and Roy Schwartz built a journalism juggernaut on this very idea. Axios, named after the Greek word for "worthy," was launched in 2017 to be a "mix between *The Economist* and Twitter," distilling the latest news and analysis into bite-size morsels on the web and in its popular daily newsletters. Nearly every Axios article is exceedingly brief, broken down with layers of clear headlines and bullets, embracing our modern media consumption patterns. The concept has worked well so far, as the company has attracted more than a million email subscribers—and just sold for over half a billion dollars.[20]

These scannable designs make use of what designers call *hierarchy*. Through typography, color, size, and placement, a layout with effective visual hierarchy immediately tells you

Figure 8.5. Our default mode to read on a
screen is by skimming and jumping.

where to focus your attention. Bold text is more noticeable
than light text. Bright colors jump to our eyes before cooler,
darker tones. Larger items or items surrounded by more space
stand out above smaller ones. And items placed at the top of
a layout will catch our focus before ones farther down. If we
turn these dials, we can direct attention to the parts of our
message we want in the order we want: *Read this headline first.
Then this subhead next. Then this body text last.*

We've talked of transportation and engineering meta-
phors in this chapter, and for good reason. In terms of getting

your message across visually, you'll struggle to find a simpler set of communications than the signs that line our more than 160,000 miles of highways in the United States.

When you're hurtling down the interstate at seventy miles per hour, you're going more than one hundred feet a second—so it's vital that any messages about directions, road conditions, or regulations get to the point quickly and clearly. Right there on the first page of the Federal Highway Administration's bible for road signs, the *Manual on Uniform Traffic Control Devices* (a thrilling read), is a set of five guidelines for doing just that.[21]

> To be effective, a traffic control device should meet five basic requirements:
>
> + Fulfill a need.
> + Command attention.
> + Convey a clear, simple meaning.
> + Command respect from road users.
> + Give adequate time for proper response.

This is a fitting place to end this chapter—with rules for designing and communicating at highway speed. There's no room for fluff when your exit is quickly coming up, and today's loud and demanding world unfortunately resembles a highway more often than not. If we want our audience to get where we want them to go, we could all take a hint from these principles. Design accordingly.

The Work

- If each word costs you $10, how many could you cut? What about $1,000?
- If you had to distill your message down to a road sign, what would it look like?
- Can your message be understood over the phone? Can it be understood in a crowded bar?
- Would a receiver need any prior knowledge to understand your message? Will all your receivers have this knowledge?
- Play Jenga with your message. How many pieces can you pull out before it comes crashing down?

CONCLUSION

What's Next?

*Everything should be made as simple
as possible, but not simpler.*

—Albert Einstein

In the rapidly modernizing postwar America of the 1950s, convenience was king. Miracle products promised marvels of the modern world, and futurists were predicting that soon "people will live in houses so automatic that push-buttons will be replaced by fingertip and even voice controls."[1]

The wizards at General Mills introduced a product that sounded like one of those miracles: instant cake mix. Simply open the box, pour the powder into a bowl, and add water. A couple of stirs followed by a few minutes in a hot oven and within minutes you have a beautiful "homemade" cake.

Except, homemakers *hated* it.

Betty Crocker's instant cake mix was *too* easy. After being conditioned to laboriously bake their sweets from scratch, people felt like they were cheating when opening up a box and adding some water. The mix produced perfect cakes and garnered plenty of praise—but that praise turned into guilt. The bakers didn't make that cake. The factory did.

When the company tried to figure out how to solve this, they unearthed a counterintuitive solution: make it more complicated. Instead of including an egg in powdered form, they asked bakers to crack and add their own. They added a step.

Water is cheating—but an egg is cooking. Adding that slight bit of work transformed how customers looked at the process, the product, and their relationship with both. The pride they took is an example of a phenomenon known as the *instrumentality heuristic.*

Throughout this book we've looked at how simplicity and fluency make things easier and more effective, and a mountain of evidence supports that. But what instrumentality tells us is that when we are actively pursuing a goal, such as baking a cake in the case of General Mills or earning a doctorate after writing a tough dissertation, we value something more when it takes more effort.[2] When we work harder for something we want, ultimately, it means more to us. As Theodore Roosevelt said, "Nothing in the world is worth having or worth doing unless it means effort, pain, difficulty."

Simplicity is how we push through the noise and the indifference. But complication, when done right, can have a home in our toolbox. The secret is, complexity is a tool that works only when we're motivated. It works only to pull us closer to something we already want. It can't push, only pull. The researchers that pioneered the instrumentality heuristic, Aparna A. Labroo and Sara Kim from the University of Chicago, put it plainly: "In all previous research, ease of processing increased liking of an object, whereas in the studies reported here, difficulty of processing increased liking of an object provided the object was a means to reach a current goal."

Unfortunately, as marketers, entrepreneurs, educators, advocates, or anybody else with a message that needs to be heard, we don't always have this luxury. That's where the lessons from the leaders, innovators, and scientists in this book come to bear.

Google's spartan home page has been largely unchanged since it first went online in 1998. In that time, it's become the ultimate tool, with email and calendars, documents and spreadsheets, movie times and stock prices. Starting with that little text box, we can do anything.

Tech executive Marissa Mayer, who later went on to lead Yahoo and other companies, started her career as employee number twenty at Google and soon took charge of the site's look and feel. In 2005, as the company was in the midst of growing into a global superpower, she described her challenge: "Google has the functionality of a really complicated Swiss Army knife, but the home page is our way of approaching it closed. It's simple, it's elegant, you can slip it in your pocket, but it's got the great doodad when you need it. A lot of our competitors are like a Swiss Army knife open—and that can be intimidating and occasionally harmful."[3]

Intimidating and harmful. We want to accomplish our goals, and we like products, ideas, and people that help us do that—not those that are intimidating and harmful. That's the result of complication, and that's the line we must not cross.

Simplicity requires certainty, or at least conviction. This is essential in many areas of life and business but foolishly misguided in others. Life is meant to be an uncertain adventure; our future is unwritten and big and mysterious. We can't know everything, and we shouldn't know everything—and simplicity is certainly not the answer for everything.

But one big thing we know for sure. Reaching out, connecting, and being truly heard is one of the best, most rewarding parts of that fuzzy, unknown, and unpredictable life.

Start-ups, like Google once was, desperately seek a state known as *product-market fit* in their business. That's the moment when what you are selling is what the customers actually want to buy—when it all clicks. They test, iterate, pivot, improve, and look under every rock until they find it. This process is the hardest part of building a business. But when they do find that fit, everything changes. It creates the moment of lift.

Simplicity is about finding that very fit in your message.

Why Do Some Messages Work When Others Don't?

We started this book with a problem—"why do some messages work when others don't"—and ended it by equipping ourselves to face it. In the first half, we identified the challenges in our communication crisis: our squishy brains and the noisy world those brains created. We saw how fundamentally challenging it is to successfully connect from sender to receiver, and then we indicted the culprit: complication. Complication, artificially created complexity, is selfish, cowardly, and dangerous—but, unfortunately, it's in our nature.

But then, science and history gave us the tool to win this fight: simplicity.

Beneficial messages prioritize the receiver. Focused messages narrow in on telling a single story. Salient messages stand out in a crowded world. Empathetic messages show understanding. Minimal messages are designed with intention. Taken together, simple messages allow us to inform, persuade, and connect in a world that so often pushes back the other way.

What's Next?

We've looked at our history of space exploration a couple of times in our examination of connection and simplicity because it represents one of the most complex endeavors our species has ever undertaken. In that grand legacy, you'll find the most ambitious communication attempt of all time—our first effort to reach beyond our world. Stamped into a twelve-inch disc of gold-plated copper is a message that is simultaneously the farthest, fastest, and most enduring evidence of humankind that has ever been created.

Carried aboard the *Voyager 1* spacecraft is the Golden Record, a message-in-a-bottle data time capsule that features sounds and images meant to portray the variety and beauty of life on Earth.[4] On the record are recordings of Bach and Mozart, Chuck Berry's "Johnny B. Goode," Azerbaijani folk music, human brain waves, and humpback whale songs. There are images of Isaac Newton's work, Jane Goodall studying chimpanzees, the Taj Mahal, and a woman snacking on grapes in a grocery store. On the cover is an interstellar map locating Earth and a sample of slowly decaying uranium that, together, can be used to pinpoint where and when this peculiar artifact is from.

After its launch in 1977, *Voyager 1* weaved around the planets of our solar system, uncovering secrets of our planetary neighbors for the first time, and eventually whipped past Saturn into interstellar space. Nearly a half century later, the craft is miraculously still working, faithfully sending back data from almost 15 billion miles away, all while speeding farther away from us at a brisk 38,210 miles an hour.

This spacecraft is the most distant object we have ever shot into space and the farthest our species has ever reached. And, millions of years after the sun dies and swallows Earth in a giant ball of fire, it will last longer than anything else we've ever done. Carl Sagan, the astronomer behind the Golden Record attached to *Voyager's* side, described it as "destined to wander forever in the great ocean between the stars."

The record itself passes our simplicity test. It's beneficial, a buoy in the galactic ocean to show the receiver they're not alone. It's focused, designed as a time capsule to memorialize life on Earth. It's salient, printed on a shimmering disc in the dark emptiness of space. It's empathetic, labeled with universal instructions that require only vision and math. And it's minimal, a single, condensed package distilled from a planet's worth of experience.

If we're lucky, perhaps thousands, or millions, of years in the future, an alien ship will come across this artifact of our little blue planet. Setting it on a turntable, the extraterrestrial discoverer of the record will hear first a greeting in one of our oldest languages, Sumerian, ◈ 𒌋𒌋 𒊒𒁹𒌋 ⊢ 𒅘, which, when translated, is the simple message, "May all be well."

Across an inconceivable expanse of space and time, the first message from our planet to another is just one simple idea: we care about the receiver.

In our own lives here on planet Earth, we must do the same. Simplicity is an act of care, and it's the way we move forward.

Notes

Introduction

1. John Koenig, "Sonder," *Dictionary of Obscure Sorrows*, July 22, 2012, dictionaryofobscuresorrows.com/post/23536922667/sonder.

2. eMarketer, "Time Spent per Day with Digital versus Traditional Media in the United States from 2011 to 2023 (in Minutes)," *Statista*, June 6, 2021, statista-com.remote.baruch.cuny.edu /statistics/565628/time-spent-digital-traditional-media-usa/.

Chapter 1

1. Linda Rodriguez McRobbie, "Total Recall: The People Who Never Forget," *Guardian*, February 8, 2017, theguardian.com/science /2017/feb/08/total-recall-the-people-who-never-forget.

2. Daniel J. Simons and Christopher F. Chabris, "Gorillas in Our Midst: Sustained Inattentional Blindness for Dynamic Events," *Perception* 28, no. 9 (September 1999): 1059–1074, doi.org/10.1068 /p281059.

3. Siri Carpenter, "Sights Unseen," *Monitor*, American Psychological Association, April 2001, apa.org/monitor/apr01/blindness.

4. Jane Porter, "You're More Biased Than You Think," *Fast Company*, October 6, 2014, fastcompany.com/3036627/youre-more -biased-than-you-think.

5. William James, *The Principles of Psychology* (New York: Henry Holt and Company, 1890).

6. Maurice Possley, "Lydell Grant," National Registry of Exonerations, January 26, 2022, law.umich.edu/special/exoneration/Pages /casedetail.aspx?caseid=5980.

7. "Ronald Cotton," Innocence Project, August 6, 2019, innocenceproject.org/cases/ronald-cotton/; "Ryan Matthews," Innocence Project, August 9, 2019, innocenceproject.org/cases /ryan-matthews/; "DNA Exonerations in the United States (1989– 2020)," Innocence Project, August 26, 2020, innocenceproject.org /dna-exonerations-in-the-united-states/.

8. Nelson Cowan, "Chapter 20 What Are the Differences between Long-Term, Short-Term, and Working Memory?," *Progress in Brain Research* 169 (March 2008): 323–338, doi.org/10.1016 /s0079-6123(07)00020-9.

9. George A. Miller, "The Magical Number Seven, Plus or Minus Two: Some Limits on Our Capacity for Processing Information," *Psychological Review* 63, no. 2 (1956): 81–97, doi.org/10.1037 /h0043158.

10. Nelson Cowan, "The Magical Number 4 in Short-Term Memory: A Reconsideration of Mental Storage Capacity," *Behavioral and Brain Sciences* 24, no. 1 (February 2001): 87–114, doi.org /10.1017/s0140525x01003922; Richard Schweickert and Brian Boruff, "Short-Term Memory Capacity: Magic Number or Magic Spell?," *Journal of Experimental Psychology: Learning, Memory, and Cognition* 12, no. 3 (July 1986): 419–425, doi.org/10.1037/0278 -7393.12.3.419.

11. Hal Arkowitz and Scott O. Lilienfeld, "Why Science Tells Us Not to Rely on Eyewitness Accounts," *Scientific American*, January 1, 2010, scientificamerican.com/article/do-the-eyes-have-it/.

12. Leonid Rozenblit and Frank Keil, "The Misunderstood Limits of Folk Science: An Illusion of Explanatory Depth," *Cognitive Science* 26, no. 5 (September 2002): 521–562, doi.org/10.1207 /s15516709cog2605_1.

13. "Could You Win a Point off Serena Williams? Plus, Avoiding Hen/Stag Parties, and Being Naked Results," *YouGov*, July 12, 2019, yougov.co.uk/opi/surveys/results#/survey/344ce84b-a48d-11e9 -8e40-79d1f09423a3/question/4d73bd62-a48f-11e9-aee6-6742 cfe83f15/gender.

14. SellCell.com, "How Much Time on Average Do You Spend on Your Phone on a Daily Basis?," *Statista*, February 11, 2021,

statista-com.remote.baruch.cuny.edu/statistics/1224510
/time-spent-per-day-on-smartphone-us/.

15. eMarketer, "Time Spent per Day with Digital versus
Traditional Media in the United States from 2011 to 2023 (in
Minutes)," *Statista*, June 6, 2021, statista-com.remote.baruch.cuny
.edu/statistics/565628/time-spent-digital-traditional-media-usa/.

16. Ann Blair, "Information Overload's 2,300-Year-Old
History," *Harvard Business Review*, July 23, 2014, hbr.org/2011
/03/information-overloads-2300-yea.html.

17. Donald A. Norman, *Emotional Design: Why We Love (or
Hate) Everyday Things* (New York: Basic Books, 2005).

18. Peter Just, "Time and Leisure in the Elaboration of Culture,"
Journal of Anthropological Research 36, no. 1 (1980): 105–115,
jstor.org/stable/3629555; "How Many Emails Does the Average
Person Receive per Day?," *Campaign Monitor*, December 8, 2021,
campaignmonitor.com/resources/knowledge-base/how-many
-emails-does-the-average-person-receive-per-day/; Artyom Dogtiev,
"Push Notifications Statistics," *Business of Apps*, January 16, 2023,
businessofapps.com/marketplace/push-notifications/research/push
-notifications-statistics/.

19. Philipp Lorenz-Spreen et al. "Accelerating Dynamics of
Collective Attention," *Nature Communications* 10, no. 1 (April 15,
2019), doi.org/10.1038/s41467-019-09311-w.

20. Jon Gitlin, "74% of People Are Tired of Social Media
Ads—but They're Effective," *SurveyMonkey*, 2022, surveymonkey
.com/curiosity/74-of-people-are-tired-of-social-media-ads-but
-theyre-effective/; eMarketer, "Most Annoying Types of Digital Ads
according to Internet Users in the United States as of July 2019,"
Statista, August 23, 2019, statista-com.remote.baruch.cuny.edu
/statistics/257972/most-annoying-types-of-online-ads-in-the-us/.

21. Kara Pernice, "Banner Blindness Revisited: Users Dodge Ads
on Mobile and Desktop," *Nielsen Norman Group*, April 22, 2018,
nngroup.com/articles/banner-blindness-old-and-new-findings/.

Chapter 2

1. Elizabeth P. Derryberry et al. "Singing in a Silent Spring: Birds Respond to a Half-Century Soundscape Reversion during the COVID-19 Shutdown," *Science* 370, no. 6516 (September 30, 2020): 575–579, doi.org/10.1126/science.abd5777.

2. Adam L. Alter and Daniel M. Oppenheimer, "Predicting Short-Term Stock Fluctuations by Using Processing Fluency," *Proceedings of the National Academy of Sciences of the United States of America* 103, no. 24 (2006): 9369–9372, jstor.org/stable/30051949.

3. Simon M. Laham, Peter Koval, and Adam L. Alter, "The Name-Pronunciation Effect: Why People Like Mr. Smith More Than Mr. Colquhoun," *Journal of Experimental Social Psychology* 48, no. 3 (May 2012): 752–756, doi.org/10.1016/j.jesp.2011.12.002.

4. Rolf Reber, Piotr Winkielman, and Norbert Schwarz, "Effects of Perceptual Fluency on Affective Judgments," *Psychological Science* 9, no. 1 (1998): 45–48, doi.org/10.1111/1467-9280.00008.

5. Michael Ventura, *Applied Empathy: The New Language of Leadership* (New York: Atria, 2018).

6. Phil Gibbs, "What Is Occam's Razor?," UC Riverside Department of Mathematics, 1997, math.ucr.edu/home/baez/physics/General/occam.html.

7. Jura Koncius, "The Tidying Tide: Marie Kondo Effect Hits Sock Drawers and Consignment Stores," *Washington Post*, January 15, 2019, washingtonpost.com/lifestyle/home/the-tidying-tide-marie-kondo-effect-hits-sock-drawers-and-consignment-stores/2019/01/10/234e0b62-1378-11e9-803c-4ef28312c8b9_story.html.

8. Dieter Rams, "The Power of Good Design," Vitsoe, accessed April 13, 2023, vitsoe.com/us/about/good-design.

9. Cyriaque Lamar, "The 22 Rules of Storytelling, according to Pixar," *Gizmodo*, June 8, 2012, gizmodo.com/the-22-rules-of-storytelling-according-to-pixar-5916970.

10. Daniel B. Schneider, "F.Y.I.," *New York Times*, September 22, 1996, nytimes.com/1996/09/22/nyregion/fyi-419478.html.

11. Corey Kilgannon, "Decoding Parking-Sign Legalese," *New York Times*, January 17, 1999, nytimes.com/1999/01/17/nyregion/neighborhood-report-upper-east-side-decoding-parking-sign-legalese.html.

12. "Time Media Kit," *Time*, 2023, time.com/mediakit/.

13. Seb Joseph and Ronan Shields, "The Rundown: Google, Meta and Amazon Are on Track to Absorb More Than 50% of All Ad Money in 2022," *Digiday*, February 7, 2022, digiday.com/marketing/the-rundown-google-meta-and-amazon-are-on-track-to-absorb-more-than-50-of-all-ad-money-in-2022/.

14. Garson O'Toole, "One-Half the Money I Spend for Advertising Is Wasted, but I Have Never Been Able to Decide Which Half," *Quote Investigator*, April 30, 2022, quoteinvestigator.com/2022/04/11/advertising/.

15. Madeline King and Daniel Alonso, "As the Pandemic Makes Life More Complex, People Crave Simpler Brands," *Siegel+Gale*, December 15, 2021, siegelgale.com/as-the-pandemic-makes-life-more-complex-people-crave-simpler-brands/.

16. Cheri H. Ahern et al., *Youth Tobacco Surveillance—United States, 1998–1999* (Atlanta, GA: Centers for Disease Control and Prevention, October 13, 2000), cdc.gov/mmwr/preview/mmwrhtml/ss4910a1.htm; "Tobacco Use among Children and Teens," *American Lung Association*, November 17, 2022, lung.org/quit-smoking/smoking-facts/tobacco-use-among-children.

17. Matthew C. Farrelly et al. "Getting to the Truth: Evaluating National Tobacco Countermarketing Campaigns," *American Journal of Public Health* 92, no. 6 (June 2002): 901–907, doi.org/10.2105/ajph.92.6.901; "Youth and Tobacco Use," Centers for Disease Control and Prevention, November 10, 2022, cdc.gov/tobacco/data_statistics/fact_sheets/youth_data/tobacco_use/index.htm.

Chapter 3

1. United States Office of Strategic Services, *Simple Sabotage Field Manual* (Washington, DC: Office of Strategic Services, 1944), gutenberg.org/cache/epub/26184/pg26184-images.html.

2. "Complexity Bias: Why We Prefer Complicated to Simple," *Farnam Street* (blog), June 6, 2020, fs.blog/complexity-bias/.

3. Hilary H. Farris and Russell Revlin, "Sensible Reasoning in Two Tasks: Rule Discovery and Hypothesis Evaluation," *Memory & Cognition* 17, no. 2 (March 1989): 221–232, doi.org/10.3758/bf03197071.

4. Leidy Klotz, *Subtract: The Untapped Science of Less* (New York: Flatiron Books, 2021).

5. "Terms of Service; Didn't Read," accessed April 13, 2023, tosdr.org/.

6. "Visualizing the Length of the Fine Print, for 14 Popular Apps," *Business Insider*, April 18, 2020, markets.businessinsider.com/news/stocks/terms-of-service-visualizing-the-length-of-internet-agreements-1029104238.

7. George Orwell, "Politics and the English Language," Orwell Foundation, originally published in *Horizon* April 1946, accessed April 13, 2023, orwellfoundation.com/the-orwell-foundation/orwell/essays-and-other-works/politics-and-the-english-language/.

8. Hun-Tong Tan, Elaine Ying Wang, and G-Song Yoo, "Who Likes Jargon? The Joint Effect of Jargon Type and Industry Knowledge on Investors' Judgments," *Journal of Accounting and Economics* 67, no. 2–3 (2019): 416–437, doi.org/10.1016/j.jacceco.2019.03.001.

9. Lokman I. Meho, "The Rise and Rise of Citation Analysis," *Physics World* 20, no. 1 (2007): 32–36, doi.org/10.1088/2058-7058/20/1/33.

10. Adam Conner-Simons, "How Three MIT Students Fooled the World of Scientific Journals," *MIT News*, Massachusetts Institute of Technology, April 14, 2015, news.mit.edu/2015/how-three-mit-students-fooled-scientific-journals-0414; Matan Shelomi, "Opinion: Using Pokémon to Detect Scientific Misinformation," *Scientist*, November 1, 2020, the-scientist.com/critic-at-large/opinion-using-pokmon-to-detect-scientific-misinformation-68098.

11. John Scalzi, "Teching the Tech," *Whatever: Furiously Reasonable*, October 13, 2009, whatever.scalzi.com/2009/10/13/teching-the-tech/.

12. Edward Tufte, "PowerPoint Does Rocket Science—and Better Techniques for Technical Reports," Edward Tufte Forum, 2006, edwardtufte.com/bboard/q-and-a-fetch-msg?msg_id=0001yB.

13. Dale Wilson, "Failure to Communicate," *Flight Safety Foundation*, October 20, 2016, flightsafety.org/asw-article/failure-to -communicate/; Joint Commission International, *Communicating Clearly and Effectively to Patients: How to Overcome Common Communication Challenges in Health Care*, 2018, store.jointcommission international.org/assets/3/7/jci-wp-communicating-clearly-final _(1).pdf.

14. Tren Griffin, *Charlie Munger: The Complete Investor* (New York: Columbia University Press, 2015), 52.

15. Noel Tichy and Ram Charan, "Speed, Simplicity, Self-Confidence: An Interview with Jack Welch," *Harvard Business Review*, March 3, 2020, hbr.org/1989/09/speed-simplicity-self-confidence -an-interview-with-jack-welch.

16. Byoung-Hyoun Hwang and Hugh Hoikwang Kim, "It Pays to Write Well," *Journal of Financial Economics* 124, no. 2 (May 2017): 373–394, doi.org/10.1016/j.jfineco.2017.01.006.

Chapter 4

1. Paul Dickson, "Sputnik's Impact on America," PBS, November 6, 2007, pbs.org/wgbh/nova/article/sputnik-impact-on-america/.

2. Allie Hutchison, "50 Years Ago, One Speech Revolutionized the Space Age and Took Us to the Moon," *Inverse*, September 12, 2022, inverse.com/science/50-years-ago-one-speech-revolutionized-the -space-age-took-us-to-the-moon.

3. John F. Kennedy, "Address at Rice University on the Nation's Space Effort," September 12, 1962, Rice University, transcript and video, JFK Library, jfklibrary.org/learn/about-jfk/historic-speeches /address-at-rice-university-on-the-nations-space-effort.

4. Clayton M. Christensen, Scott Cook, and Taddy Hall, "What Customers Want from Your Products," *Working Knowledge*, Harvard Business School, January 16, 2006, hbswk.hbs.edu/item/what -customers-want-from-your-products.

5. American Heart Association, "How Much Sugar Is Too Much?," American Heart Association, June 2, 2022, heart.org/en/healthy-living/healthy-eating/eat-smart/sugar/how-much-sugar-is-too-much.

6. Eleni Mantzari et al. "Public Support for Policies to Improve Population and Planetary Health: A Population-Based Online Experiment Assessing Impact of Communicating Evidence of Multiple versus Single Benefits," *Social Science & Medicine* 296 (March 2022): 114726, doi.org/10.1016/j.socscimed.2022.114726.

7. A. H. Maslow, "A Theory of Human Motivation," *Psychological Review* 50, no. 4 (1943): 370–396, doi.org/10.1037/h0054346.

8. "Black+Decker 20v Max* PowerConnect Cordless Drill/Driver + 30 pc. Kit (LD120VA)," Amazon, accessed March 16, 2023, amazon.com/decker-ld120va-20-volt-lithium-accessories/dp/b006v6yapi?th=1#:–:text=product%20description-,the,-black%2bdecker%2020v.

Chapter 5

1. Mary Shelley, *Frankenstein; or, the Modern Prometheus* (London, UK, 1818; Project Gutenberg, 2022), chap. 5, gutenberg.org/cache/epub/84/pg84-images.html.

2. Jason M. Watson and David L. Strayer, "Supertaskers: Profiles in Extraordinary Multitasking Ability," *Psychonomic Bulletin & Review* 17, no. 4 (August 2010): 479–485, doi.org/10.3758/pbr.17.4.479.

3. Brian Mullen, Craig Johnson, and Eduardo Salas, "Productivity Loss in Brainstorming Groups: A Meta-Analytic Integration," *Basic and Applied Social Psychology* 12, no. 1 (March 1991): 3–23, doi.org/10.1207/s15324834basp1201_1; Tomas Chamorro-Premuzic, "Why Group Brainstorming Is a Waste of Time," *Harvard Business Review*, March 25, 2015, hbr.org/2015/03/why-group-brainstorming-is-a-waste-of-time.

4. David Ogilvy, *Ogilvy on Advertising* (New York: Vintage Books, 1985).

5. Bruce Springsteen, *Born to Run* (New York: Simon & Schuster, 2016).

6. Leidy Klotz, *Subtract: The Untapped Science of Less* (New York: Flatiron Books, 2021).

7. "Rumor Has It . . . Office Politics Exist," Robert Half Talent Solutions, June 29, 2016, press.roberthalf.com/2016-06-29-Rumor -Has-It-Office-Politics-Exist.

8. Rory Sutherland, *Alchemy: The Dark Art and Curious Science of Creating Magic in Brands, Business, and Life* (New York: HarperCollins, 2019).

9. Neil Patel, "Your Secret Mental Weapon: 'Don't Let the Perfect Be the Enemy of the Good,'" *Entrepreneur*, August 31, 2015, entrepreneur.com/living/your-secret-mental-weapon-dont-let-the -perfect-be-the/249676.

10. "Origins and Construction of the Eiffel Tower," La Tour Eiffel Paris, accessed January 4, 2022, toureiffel.paris/en/the-monument /history.

Chapter 6

1. Trip Gabriel, "'Oh, Jane, See How Popular We Are,'" *New York Times*, October 3, 1996, nytimes.com/1996/10/03/garden/oh-jane -see-how-popular-we-are.html.

2. "Dr. Seuss: The Story behind 'The Cat in the Hat,'" Biography, June 4, 2020, biography.com/news/story-behind-dr-seuss-cat-in -the-hat.

3. "The Cat in the Hat," Dr. Seuss Wiki, February 2, 2023, seuss .fandom.com/wiki/The_Cat_in_the_Hat.

4. Ellis Conklin, "Theodor Geisel, Dr. Seuss Doing in Dick and Jane," United Press International, September 14, 1986, upi.com /Archives/1986/09/14/Theodor-Geisel-Dr-Seuss-Doing-in-Dick -and-Jane/6252527054400/.

5. Bernard Marius 't Hart et al. "Attention in Natural Scenes: Contrast Affects Rapid Visual Processing and Fixations Alike," *Philosophical Transactions of the Royal Society B: Biological Sciences* 368, no. 1628 (October 19, 2013): 20130067, doi.org/10.1098

/rstb.2013.0067; Douglas S. Brungart, "Informational and Energetic Masking Effects in the Perception of Two Simultaneous Talkers," *Journal of the Acoustical Society of America* 109, no. 3 (March 2001): 1101–1109, doi.org/10.1121/1.1345696.

6. Rolf Reber, Piotr Winkielman, and Norbert Schwarz, "Effects of Perceptual Fluency on Affective Judgments," *Psychological Science* 9, no. 1 (May 6, 1998): 45–48, doi.org/10.1111/1467-9280.00008; Nathan Novemsky et al. "Preference Fluency in Choice," *Journal of Marketing Research* 44, no. 3 (October 16, 2007): 347–356, doi.org/10.1509/jmkr.44.3.347.

7. Henry Jaglom, *The Movie Business Book* (New York: Simon & Schuster, 1992).

8. Robert B. Cialdini, *Influence: The Psychology of Persuasion* (New York: Collins, 2007).

9. [Cicero], *Rhetorica ad Herennium*, book IV, 47–69 (Cambridge, MA, 1954; University of Chicago, accessed April 13, 2023), penelope.uchicago.edu/Thayer/E/Roman/Texts/Rhetorica_ad _Herennium/4C*.html.

10. Lassi A. Liikkanen et al. "Time Constraints in Design Idea Generation," (lecture, 17th International Conference on Engineering Design, Palo Alto, CA, August 2009).

11. Elise Harris, "Pope Tells Priests to Keep Homilies Brief: 'No More Than 10 Minutes!'," *Catholic News Agency*, February 7, 2018, catholicnewsagency.com/news/37706/pope-tells-priests-to-keep -homilies-brief-no-more-than-10-minutes.

12. Fatnick, "The Mysterious Legacy of the SNES Soundchip," Fatnick Industries, August 19, 2016, mechafatnick.co.uk/2016/08 /19/the-mysterious-legacy-of-the-snes-soundchip/.

13. Lorraine Boissoneault, "A Brief History of the GIF, from Early Internet Innovation to Ubiquitous Relic," *Smithsonian*, June 2, 2017, smithsonianmag.com/history/brief-history-gif-early-internet -innovation-ubiquitous-relic-180963543/.

Chapter 7

1. Eytan Bakshy, Solomon Messing, and Lada A. Adamic, "Exposure to Ideologically Diverse News and Opinion on Facebook," *Science* 348, no. 6239 (May 2015): 1130–1132, doi.org/10.1126 /science.aaa1160.

2. Cameron J. Bunker and Michael E. W. Varnum, "How Strong Is the Association between Social Media Use and False Consensus?," *Computers in Human Behavior* 125 (December 2021): 106947, doi.org/10.1016/j.chb.2021.106947.

3. Lee Ross, David Greene, and Pamela House, "The 'False Consensus Effect': An Egocentric Bias in Social Perception and Attribution Processes," *Journal of Experimental Social Psychology* 13, no. 3 (May 1977): 279–301, doi.org/10.1016/0022-1031(77) 90049-x.

4. Ross, Greene, and House, "The 'False Consensus Effect.'"

5. Roseanna Sommers and Vanessa K. Bohns, "The Voluntariness of Voluntary Consent: Consent Searches and the Psychology of Compliance," *Yale Law Journal* 128, no. 7 (April 10, 2019): 1962–2033, ssrn.com/abstract=3369844.

6. *Women in the Workplace 2021*, McKinsey & Company and Lean In, womenintheworkplace.com/2021; Kiara Taylor, "America's Top Black CEOs," *Investopedia*, June 25, 2022, investopedia.com /top-black-ceos-5220330.

7. "Glassdoor's Diversity and Inclusion Workplace Survey," *Glassdoor*, September 29, 2020, glassdoor.com/blog/glassdoors -diversity-and-inclusion-workplace-survey/.

8. Sylvia Ann Hewlett, Melinda Marshall, and Laura Sherbin, "How Diversity Can Drive Innovation," *Harvard Business Review*, August 1, 2014, hbr.org/2013/12/how-diversity-can-drive -innovation.

9. Gallup, "How Does Gallup Polling Work?," Gallup, October 20, 2014, news.gallup.com/poll/101872/how-does-gallup-polling-work .aspx.

10. Paul Graham, "What I've Learned from Users," *Paul Graham* (blog) September 2022, paulgraham.com/users.html.

11. Teresa M. Amabile and Mukti Khaire, "Creativity and the Role of the Leader," *Harvard Business Review*, October 2008, hbr.org /2008/10/creativity-and-the-role-of-the-leader; Gino Cattani and Simone Ferriani, "How Outsiders Become Game Changers," *Harvard Business Review*, August 5, 2021, hbr.org/2021/08/how-outsiders -become-game-changers.

12. Tom Kelley, "The Ten Faces of Innovation," IDEO, October 2005, ideo.com/post/the-ten-faces-of-innovation.

13. Ellie Violet Bramley, "Desire Paths: The Illicit Trails That Defy the Urban Planners," *Guardian*, October 5, 2018, theguardian .com/cities/2018/oct/05/desire-paths-the-illicit-trails-that-defy-the -urban-planners.

14. Richard Priday, "The Inside Story of the Great KFC Chicken Shortage of 2018," *Wired*, February 21, 2018, wired.co.uk/article/kfc -chicken-crisis-shortage-supply-chain-logistics-experts.

15. Seth Godin, "Talker's Block," *Seth's Blog*, September 23, 2011, seths.blog/2011/09/talkers-block/.

Chapter 8

1. Alexander Burns and Maggie Haberman, "Republican Hopefuls Jockey for 2016," *Politico*, August 10, 2012, politico.com/story/2012 /08/republican-hopefuls-jockey-for-2016-079541.

2. *Knock Down the House*, directed by Rachel Lears, aired May 1, 2019, on Netflix.

3. Marie Kondo, "Konmari Is Not Minimalism," KonMari, accessed February 15, 2023, konmari.com/konmari-is-not -minimalism/.

4. Daniel M. Oppenheimer, "Consequences of Erudite Vernacular Utilized Irrespective of Necessity: Problems with Using Long Words Needlessly," *Applied Cognitive Psychology* 20, no. 2 (March 2006): 139–156, doi.org/10.1002/acp.1178.

5. *Data Point: Adult Literacy in the United States* (Washington, DC: US Department of Education, July 2019); Saida Mamedova, Dinah Sparks, and Kathleen Mulveney Hoyer, *Adult Education*

Attainment and Assessment Scores: A Cross-National Comparison, National Center for Education Statistics, US Department of Education, September 19, 2017, nces.ed.gov/pubsearch/pubsinfo .asp?pubid=2018007; "Highlights of PIAAC 2017 U.S. Results," National Center for Education Statistics, 2017, nces.ed.gov/surveys /piaac/national_results.asp.

6. Alex Moore, "7 Tips for Getting More Responses to Your Emails (with Data!)," *Boomerang* (blog), February 12, 2016, blog .boomerangapp.com/2016/02/7-tips-for-getting-more-responses -to-your-emails-with-data.

7. "Updates to the OED," Oxford English Dictionary, December 2022, public.oed.com/updates.

8. Amos Tversky and Daniel Kahneman, "Judgment under Uncertainty: Heuristics and Biases," *Science* 185, no. 4157 (1974): 1124–1131, jstor.org/stable/1738360.

9. Martin Gardner, "The Ultimate Turtle," *New York Review,* June 16, 1988, nybooks.com/articles/1988/06/16/the-ultimate-turtle/.

10. James Clear, "First Principles: Elon Musk on the Power of Thinking for Yourself," *James Clear* (blog), accessed February 15, 2023, jamesclear.com/first-principles.

11. Randall Munroe, *Thing Explainer: Complicated Stuff in Simple Words* (Boston: Houghton Mifflin Harcourt, 2015).

12. "What Can the Oxford English Corpus Tell Us about the English Language," Oxford Dictionaries, August 12, 2018, en.oxforddictionaries .com/explore/what-can-corpustell-us-about-language (site discontinued).

13. George Orwell, "Politics and the English Language," Orwell Foundation, originally published in *Horizon* April 1946, accessed April 13, 2023, orwellfoundation.com/the-orwell-foundation /orwell/essays-and-other-works/politics-and-the-english-language/.

14. William Strunk and E. B. White, *The Elements of Style* (New York: Macmillan, 1959), 23.

15. Benjamin Dreyer, *Dreyer's English: An Utterly Correct Guide to Clarity and Style* (New York: Random House, 2019), chap. 12.

16. Jakob Nielsen, "How Users Read on the Web," Nielsen Norman Group, September 30, 1997, nngroup.com/articles/how -users-read-on-the-web/.

17. "New Rules of Email Marketing," *Campaign Monitor*, accessed February 15, 2023, campaignmonitor.com/resources/guides/email-marketing-new-rules/.

18. "MIT Research - Brain Processing of Visual Information," *MIT News*, Massachusetts Institute of Technology, December 19, 1996, news.mit.edu/1996/visualprocessing.

19. Kara Pernice, "Text Scanning Patterns: Eyetracking Evidence," Nielsen Norman Group, August 25, 2019, nngroup.com/articles/text-scanning-patterns-eyetracking/.

20. Alex Shephard, "Axios and Donald Trump Are Made for Each Other," *New Republic*, May 2, 2017, newrepublic.com/article/142441/axios-donald-trump-made; Benjamin Mullin, "Axios Agrees to Sell Itself to Cox Enterprises for $525 Million," *New York Times*, August 8, 2022, nytimes.com/2022/08/08/business/media/axios-cox-enterprises.html.

21. "2009 MUTCD with Revisions 1, 2, and 3 Incorporated, Dated July 2022 (PDF)," Manual on Uniform Traffic Control Devices, Federal Highway Administration, US Department of Transportation, July 2022, mutcd.fhwa.dot.gov/pdfs/2009r1r2r3/pdf_index.htm.

Conclusion

1. Matt Novak, "How Experts Think We'll Live in 2000 A.D. (1950)," *Paleofuture* (blog), January 28, 2008, paleofuture.com/blog/2008/1/28/how-experts-think-well-live-in-2000-ad-1950.html.

2. Aparna A. Labroo and Sara Kim, "The 'Instrumentality' Heuristic," *Psychological Science* 20, no. 1 (February 2009): 127–134, doi.org/10.1111/j.1467-9280.2008.02264.x.

3. Linda Tischler, "The Beauty of Simplicity," *Fast Company*, November 1, 2005, fastcompany.com/56804/beauty-simplicity.

4. "The Golden Record," Voyager, Jet Propulsion Laboratory, NASA, accessed February 15, 2023, voyager.jpl.nasa.gov/golden-record.

Resources

Communicating simply is hard work. To help you get the most out of this book, I've put together several additional resources to make it easier. Check out my website to get access to free guides, cheat sheets, checklists, and more, all at BenGuttmann.com/resources.

I hope we can keep in touch. Every week I send out a brief email with ideas from me and others, and I'd love to share it with you too. You can sign up for free at BenGuttmann.com /newsletter.

Lastly, let me know what you think of this book, ask me a question, invite me to your event, or just reach out to say hi via email at ben@benguttmann.com. I'm looking forward to hearing from you!

Acknowledgments

I have never been under the illusion that anything I've ever done has been on my own. I'm grateful to the whole universe of people and institutions that have helped make me who I am today and who ultimately make this book possible.

The team at Berrett-Koehler have all been incredible partners throughout this process, including (but not limited to) Neal Maillet, Jeevan Sivasubramaniam, Ashley Ingram, David Marshall, Sarah Nelson, and Katelyn Keating.

I am grateful to Harvey Klinger and his team for reaching out, guiding me, and representing me at every step of the way.

I wouldn't have the experiences that led to this book if it weren't for my former colleagues and friends at Digital Natives Group. We had many great people on our team through the years, but I'd be remiss if I didn't mention my longtime collaborators Vladimir Lackovic, Jonathan Jacobs, John Botte, Ellie Eckert, Bryan Trindade, Weston Gardner, and Thaiyeba Jalil. I'm also thankful to the legions of clients and partners that we worked with through our ten years, particularly several who have helped mentor me through the book writing journey: David Perlmutter, Michael Ventura, William Ury, Martin Lindstrom, and Michael Schein.

Over the years, I've had every type of ID card that the City University of New York issues: student, alumnus, staff, and faculty. I'm grateful to those who taught me as a student and to those whom I now get to teach as an educator at Baruch College. CUNY is a family affair, with both my parents and spouse all alumni, and as a New Yorker I'm proud of this one-of-a-kind public institution. And I thank the tireless and caring educators that taught me before Baruch, particularly the early mentors I had in the Smithtown School of Business.

Speaking of family, I am always grateful for the love and support of my parents, my brother, my sister, my grand-parents, and my extended family—those who are still with us and those who are not. Love you all.

And finally, I owe everything to my incredible wife, Stephania, who is by far the most beautiful and loving person I have ever met. Thank you.

Index

About the Author

Ben Guttmann is an entrepreneur, educator, and adviser who has been trusted to help tell the story of global brands including the NFL, I Love NY, and Comcast NBCUniversal. For ten years before its acquisition, he ran Digital Natives Group, an award-winning marketing agency that partnered with brands including the Nature Conservancy, Grand Central Terminal, and Swiss Re, as well as luminaries including Nobel laureates, Fortune 500 CEOs, and bestselling authors.

Ben has taught at CUNY Baruch College for nine years as a top-rated member of the marketing faculty. Among other publications, his writing or his work has been featured in the *New York Times*, *Wall Street Journal*, *Publishers Weekly*, and *Crain's New York Business*.

He's a proud New Yorker, and you can find him hosting the popular Queens Tech Night meetup, serving on the board of a number of civic organizations, or cycling around the city.

Berrett–Koehler
Publishers

Berrett-Koehler is an independent publisher dedicated to an ambitious mission: *Connecting people and ideas to create a world that works for all.*

Our publications span many formats, including print, digital, audio, and video. We also offer online resources, training, and gatherings. And we will continue expanding our products and services to advance our mission.

We believe that the solutions to the world's problems will come from all of us, working at all levels: in our society, in our organizations, and in our own lives. Our publications and resources offer pathways to creating a more just, equitable, and sustainable society. They help people make their organizations more humane, democratic, diverse, and effective (and we don't think there's any contradiction there). And they guide people in creating positive change in their own lives and aligning their personal practices with their aspirations for a better world.

And we strive to practice what we preach through what we call "The BK Way." At the core of this approach is *stewardship,* a deep sense of responsibility to administer the company for the benefit of all of our stakeholder groups, including authors, customers, employees, investors, service providers, sales partners, and the communities and environment around us. Everything we do is built around stewardship and our other core values of *quality, partnership, inclusion,* and *sustainability.*

This is why Berrett-Koehler is the first book publishing company to be both a B Corporation (a rigorous certification) and a benefit corporation (a for-profit legal status), which together require us to adhere to the highest standards for corporate, social, and environmental performance. And it is why we have instituted many pioneering practices (which you can learn about at www.bkconnection.com), including the Berrett-Koehler Constitution, the Bill of Rights and Responsibilities for BK Authors, and our unique Author Days.

We are grateful to our readers, authors, and other friends who are supporting our mission. We ask you to share with us examples of how BK publications and resources are making a difference in your lives, organizations, and communities at www.bkconnection.com/impact.

Dear reader,

Thank you for picking up this book and welcome to the worldwide BK community! You're joining a special group of people who have come together to create positive change in their lives, organizations, and communities.

What's BK all about?

Our mission is to connect people and ideas to create a world that works for all.

Why? Our communities, organizations, and lives get bogged down by old paradigms of self-interest, exclusion, hierarchy, and privilege. But we believe that can change. That's why we seek the leading experts on these challenges—and share their actionable ideas with you.

A welcome gift

To help you get started, we'd like to offer you a **free copy** of one of our bestselling ebooks:

www.bkconnection.com/welcome

When you claim your **free ebook**, you'll also be subscribed to our blog.

Our freshest insights

Access the best new tools and ideas for leaders at all levels on our blog at ideas.bkconnection.com.

Sincerely,

Your friends at Berrett-Koehler

Certified

Corporation